HURRICANES

HURRICANES

A MEMOIR

RICK ROSS

WITH NEIL MARTINEZ-BELKIN

HANOVER
SQUARE
PRESS

HANOVER
SQUARE
PRESS

ISBN-13: 978-1-335-99928-3
ISBN-13: 978-1-335-01678-2 (Barnes & Noble signed edition)
ISBN-13: 978-1-335-01679-9 (Barnes & Noble Black Friday signed edition)

Hurricanes

Library of Congress Cataloging-in-Publication Data has been applied for.

HanoverSqPress.com
BookClubbish.com

Printed in U.S.A.

This book is dedicated to my big brother. Carol City.

HURRICANES

PROLOGUE

SOMETHING WAS GOING ON OUTSIDE. THE
Dobermans were barking. I rolled out of bed and walked to the
foyer. Out the window I saw them. A SWAT team gathered at
the bottom of the hill. It looked to be about twenty of them.
They were suited up and ready to kill. They had rifles. They
had shotguns. They had battering rams and bulletproof shields.
And they were cutting the gates to the studio house.

It was a full house that morning. Lira was still sleeping in my
room. Toie was in hers. She was having a sleepover with her
sister Lashiain, her cousin Jocelyn, her friend Isis, and Kano's
two daughters, Kerina and Jenyea. Black was in his room. Slab
was on the couch in the living room. My homie Short Legs,
Scrilla and my videographer Ryan were all downstairs in the
basement. Meek and Nicki had been there the night before but
it looked like they had left.

I woke Black and Slab up and told them to flush the weed

and hide the guns. While they argued about whether or not to unlock the front door I went back into my room. I was going to pretend to be asleep.

Slab ended up opening the doors. They slammed him to the ground and put a knee in his back. When they busted into my room moments later I noticed two things. The first was the cluster of green dots. Lasers from the assault rifles pointed at my chest. Then I saw the words printed across their tactical gear.

US Marshals. Southeast Regional Fugitive Task Force.

The feds?

"Hands in the air! Everybody on the ground!"

I put my hands in the air. I got on the ground.

"How many people are in the house?!"

"I don't know but my daughter and her friends are upstairs," I said. "Don't do anything reckless."

Room by room, they started rounding everybody up. When they went downstairs Short Legs wouldn't come out from the corner of the basement he was tucked away in. He seemed unfazed. They had to throw a flash grenade at him to get him to come out.

I was cuffed and taken outside, where I was made to lie face-down in the grass of my front yard. I could hear Black's voice behind me. He was going bad on the marshal in charge. I believe his name was Jim.

"Black, stay with the girls," I shouted. "Whatever this shit is about, I'll be out soon."

"I can't, Fatboy," he called back. "They're here for me too."

When I realized they'd come for Black too I started to get an idea what this was about. But it still didn't explain why the *feds* had come. That part was throwing me off and it was concerning. I wondered if I should have Renee move the money into her account.

Everybody was outside by then. Short Legs had overheard Black and I talking and he said he'd drive the girls back to Miami. Lira was in tears. Slab was giving the agents a fake name and they hadn't even asked him shit. I'd had Ryan in the basement working around the clock for so long he was probably relieved to be getting a break.

Two of the marshals snatched me up off the ground and escorted me down the driveway. As we made our way I looked back at Toie. She was in shock. She didn't know what was happening. But Kano's daughters did. Three years earlier their father was taken away by the feds. Kano got caught up in a sting operation and they had him on a wire talking about robbing a Haitian freighter for 100 kilos. The girls hadn't seen him since.

From the back seat of a black paddy wagon I could hear the marshals talking outside. They were disappointed I'd been at the studio house. They all thought they were going to get to see the big house. The Holyfield estate.

Then I noticed a familiar face: a local cop in the crowd of US Marshals. He was the fat, bald redneck who arrested me two weeks earlier for having a couple joints in my car. He'd been waiting for me outside the big house. As soon as I pulled out the gates in my Mulsanne he'd pulled me over. It was Deputy Sheriff Tommy Grier of the Fayette County Sheriff's Office. As soon as we made eye contact he came up to the car.

"Didn't I tell you I'd see you soon?" he laughed.

Rapper Rick Ross Arrested on Suspicion of Pistol-Whipping, Kidnapping Employee

—*The Los Angeles Times*

Warrants: Man Assaulted by Rapper Rick Ross "Lost Use of Jaw"

—*The Atlanta Journal-Constitution*

Rick Ross Charged in Assault that Left Victim Unable to Chew Solid Foods

—*Fayette County News*

Black and I were taken to Fayette County Jail, and booked on charges of kidnapping, aggravated assault and aggravated battery. Both of us were denied bond and would sit behind bars until our next hearing the following week.

I spent that week in solitary confinement, locked down for twenty-three hours a day in an eight-by-twelve-foot cell. The fluorescent bulb over my head was kept on at all times. The hole is where they put inmates on suicide watch who require 24/7 visual supervision.

I refused to eat the slop they brought me. I'd spoken with my chef and she told me to just fast and stay hydrated. When they tried serving me what looked like possum or racoon stew I flipped the tray over. The red "fortified punch" that came with it spilled everywhere. I don't know what they put in that punch but it stained the floor of my cell for days. The next day they brought me a white-bread-and-pork-bologna sandwich. I told them I don't eat swine and to bring me something else. I was laughed at. When I told them they couldn't deny me food they laughed harder and claimed they had sovereign immunity. I ended up giving a correctional officer a thousand dollars to bring me some Chinese rice with sweet-and-sour chicken. By that point I was so hungry I didn't even chew it. I inhaled it.

I wanted a cell phone but that was a bad idea with my bond hearing around the corner. They had cell phone detector devices and were sending extraction teams into cells every day looking for contraband. This was not like Dade County Jail. The correctional officers ain't even allowed on the cell block there. Niggas run that joint.

She did get me some paper and a pen—another no-no in solitary—so that I could write but for the first couple days nothing came to me. I have always been a visual person and my music is inspired by seeing different things. The colorless concrete world I was in didn't offer much. But as the days turned to weeks I had to find something to occupy my time. There were only so many push-ups and sit-ups I could do and I'd already read the one Indiana Jones book I was given cover to cover. So I pulled out the wrinkled-up piece of paper I had hidden away, flattened it out and tried to get my racing thoughts out of my mind.

So many false allegations, is my image tainted?
Three weeks in the hole as if a nigga heinous
As I'm pacing in the cell all these pictures painted
All I wanted was some Belaire and a danish
Inmates gave me commissary just because I'm famous
Or is it 'cause I'm rich and I know what pain is?
Assassinate Trump like I'm Zimmerman
Now accept these words as they came from Eminem
Democratic party sentenced to the pendulum
Killing them, I voted for Andre Benjamin
Head of black music, do you know what rhythm is?
Stick your hand in the basket it gets venomous
Straight player, my chicks finish my sentences
Time to squash the beef I'll kill a nemesis
Show up at the wedding in my Timberlands
And for the record, know my best man will kill a bitch

—"Free Enterprise,"
Black Market (2015)

I wasn't the only celebrity in county jail that week. The backup vocalist on Arrested Development's 1992 single "Tennessee" was sitting in the cell across from me. That was one of Black's favorite songs. One night when I couldn't sleep I called out to her. I'd remembered an old Tupac interview from when he was doing a bid in Clinton Correctional Facility in 1995. He'd said her voice helped him get through the time. I asked her if she could sing me something to ease my soul. For the next twenty minutes, she gave me some calm. *Take me to another place. Take me to another land.*

On July 1, 2015, I was escorted into Fayette County Superior Court for my bond hearing. Standing before the Honorable Judge Tommy Hankinson, I looked like someone who just spent a week in the hole. I didn't even have clean underwear on underneath my raggedy-ass orange jumpsuit.

I wasn't too keen on having to show up to court dressed like this with an unkempt beard. I felt like that was done on purpose. To make me look like the violent dangerous criminal the prosecutors were going to try to make me out to be.

My momma had gone out and found the best criminal defense lawyer money could buy. Steve Sadow. Sadow had come up under Bobby Lee Cook, the Georgia defense attorney who inspired the TV show *Matlock*. Sadow had represented T.I. when he got caught trying to buy a bunch of machine guns and silencers a few years back. I was hoping he would be able to work some of that *Matlock* magic and make this situation go away.

Sadow proposed a $2,000,000 bond. I would put up a million dollars' worth of property as collateral and another million on top of that. $500,000 in cash and $500,000 from a bail bondsman. As to the concern that I was a flight risk, I would agree to twenty-four-hour electronic surveillance and wear a GPS ankle monitor.

All that wasn't enough for Assistant District Attorney Warren Sellers. He thought Black and I posed a threat to the community and should remain behind bars until trial. He took to the podium and laid out the state's case against me.

"Your Honor, Detective David Gunter of the Fayette County Sheriff's Office is here, and by way of proffer and stipulation among the parties, he would testify that in June of this year the Defendant William Roberts had an interest in the Holyfield estate out at 794 Highway 279 in Fayetteville, Fayette County, Georgia; that he had employed two individuals, one named Leonardo Ceceras and another named Jonathan Zamudio, as property managers of that estate.

"He employed Mr. Nadrian James, the Co-Defendant in this case, as a bodyguard. I think we have some pleadings filed by Mr. Roberts indicating that he was in charge of security at that home.

"There was a guesthouse on that property. As part of their employment, these two property managers were allowed to reside in that guest home.

"On June 7 of this year, one of those property managers, Jonathan, had a birthday and he had invited some relatives and a few individuals to come up and help him celebrate that birthday.

"Apparently, Mr. Roberts and Mr. James became upset about that. On that morning, they entered the guest home, they found Leo Ceceras there, they began to beat him about the head, and face, and body with their fists.

"Mr. William Roberts had entered that home with a Glock nine-millimeter pistol in his hand. He struck Mr. Ceceras several times in the head with that pistol and ordered everyone around to leave the residence. And these individuals that left wound up gathering outside the garage area.

"A few moments later, Defendant William Roberts exited the home with that pistol in his hand, and blood on the pistol and

his hand, followed by Mr. James and by Leo Ceceras. Leo Ceceras came out bleeding from the head in a blood-covered shirt.

"William Roberts then ordered Jonathan Zamudio back into
the home. Jonathan Zamudio refused to go and held his hands up
and started taking steps backwards when Nadrian James struck
him in the side of the head.

"Both Defendants grabbed him by the shirt, pushed him
back into the home, into the corner of a room and dragged him
into that room. They began to strike him with their fists in the
face, and head and body. And William Roberts took that nine-
millimeter Glock pistol and struck Jonathan Zamudio in the
head repeatedly with that pistol. As Jonathan would raise his
hands in defense, they would tell him to put his hands down.

"They took him back outside and William Roberts asked if
there was anyone else in the guesthouse and Jonathan answered
no. And William Roberts went back into the guesthouse, came
back out a few minutes later, and again told Jonathan Zamudio
to reenter the guesthouse. He refused and the same sort of sce-
nario played out again.

"They forcibly took him back into that home, into a different bedroom, where they beat him again in the same manner,
and took him back outside. As a result of this attack, Jonathan sustained a broken jaw, two chipped teeth, contusions
and scratches.

"And while they had him in that home, William Roberts
shoved the barrel of that pistol into Jonathan Zamudio's chest,
and told him that if he told anyone, that William Roberts would
pop a cap in him.

"Leonardo Ceceras's driver's license had been taken. It showed
the address where he and his mother lived in Miami, Florida.
He was told that they knew where he and his mother lived.

"Based upon the facts, both Defendants pose a danger to the
community; they both pose a danger of threatening witnesses.

In addition, Nadrian James has a prior felony conviction in 2007 for felony marijuana in Florida.

"He has a pending—not a suspended license case—a pending Habitual Violator charge in this count, warrant number 14-0219. The Clerk has entered that in the Tracker under the name N-A-D-R-I-O-N instead of N-A-D-R-I-A-N. So it's a little difficult to find that. But that is a pending Habitual Violator case assigned in this courtroom.

"So he has committed these offenses while he's out on a $12,500 bond from his July 19, 2014, arrest on a Habitual Violator charge.

"His criminal history reflects that he has absconded in Texas on two felony drug charges as well. So he's likely to commit other felonies while out on bond. And he's likely to not appear in court.

"For these reasons, and considering the factors in OCGA section 17-6-1, the State believes that it would be inappropriate to grant either of these Defendants bonds, and we'd ask that bond be denied."

Judge Hankinson called for a recess before announcing his decision. It was only thirty minutes but it felt longer than that. Time has a way of slowing down when you're waiting to find out if you're going home or to the chain gang. I wondered if that was the point of the recess. To make me sweat it out a little.

"They could really give me *life* behind this shit?" I asked Sadow during the break.

"I'm going to pull every trick in the book but kidnapping with serious bodily injury does carry a life sentence," Sadow said. "And you wouldn't be eligible for parole until after you'd served thirty years."

"All right," Judge Hankinson started. "With regard to the Defendant William L. Roberts, after much discussion in chambers, the Court has decided to grant the bond, based on the conditions stipulated to by Defense Counsel previously on the record.

"Anything further from either parties on the case before we move on to other cases?"

"Nothing, Your Honor. Thank you," said Assistant District Attorney Sellers.

"No, Your Honor. Thank you, sir," said Sadow.

"Thank you very much, then," said the judge. "Have a good Fourth of July."

It hadn't come easy and it most definitely hadn't come cheap. But I'd made bond. *The State of Georgia vs. William Leonard Roberts II* was just getting started but at least I would get to await my fate from home.

The irony of the judge wishing me a happy Independence Day was not lost on me. It came across as a warning. That my days of freedom were numbered and that I should enjoy them while I could. Maybe I was being paranoid but these crackers in Fayette County seemed to enjoy fucking with me.

CHAPTER

1

MIAMI IS THE SOUTHERNMOST METRO-
politan city in the United States. This is a Miami story but it
starts someplace else. About a thousand miles away, in a region
that's been called "The Most Southern Place on *Earth*." I'm not
talking about Antarctica. I'm talking about the Mississippi Delta.

I was born on January 28, 1976, in Clarksdale, Mississippi.
My parents had already moved from Mississippi to Florida a few
months prior, in the fall of '75. But a week before my momma
was due she decided to go back. Not for long. We'd all be back
in Miami a few weeks later. My momma just wanted me to
come into this world surrounded by family. In the place she
still considered home. Clarksdale. "The Golden Buckle on the
Cotton Belt."

My maternal grandparents, Tommie Fields Jr. and Rosie Lee
McAfee-Fields, were born and raised in Alligator, Mississippi,

a small town in Bolivar County. After they married in 1947, Tommie and Rosie Lee relocated to the outskirts of Shelby, Mississippi, where my granddaddy rented a forty-acre plot of farmland. These were the days of sharecropping, and with the help of some Mexicans he had working for him my granddaddy worked a cotton field. When the crops came in he'd turn over most of his haul to the white landowner as rent.

On December 27, 1950, my grandparents welcomed their first child. My momma, Tommie Ann Fields. She would soon be followed by my uncles and aunties Sammie, Erma, Larry, Edward, Brenda and Linda.

My momma grew up a real country girl in Shelby. She and her siblings would ride the neighbors' cows and explore the countryside looking for pecans to pick up off the ground. As the eldest of seven she learned to perform all the daily tasks and responsibilities that farm life consists of. She fed the hogs, picked greens from the garden and hung meats inside of the smokehouse out back. She could cut wood with a crosscut saw and was more than comfortable handling weapons. My granddaddy kept a lot of guns around. .22 target pistols. .38 Special revolvers. .357 Magnums. And those were just the handguns. There were all different types of pistols, rifles and shotguns lying around the house.

Shelby was less than an hour away from Money, Mississippi, where in August of 1955 a fourteen-year-old black boy from Chicago named Emmett Till was kidnapped from his uncle's home and murdered by two white men. His crime? Whistling at a white woman at a grocery store. A month after his body was found floating in the Tallahatchie River his two killers were acquitted on all charges.

Last night I cried tears of joy
What did we do to deserve this?

Not to dwell on the past but to keep it real
I gotta represent for Emmett Till
All the dead souls in the field
Lookin' at my Rollie it's about that time
White man had a problem with mine
And we supposed to be shy?
The revolution's televised
Bobby still on the rise

—"Tears of Joy,"
Teflon Don (2010)

My granddaddy was not a violent man nor was he a civil rights activist. He was a family man, a farmer and a quartet gospel singer in his church. But nobody was going to be snatching his babies up in the middle of the night. If a mob of Ku Klux Klansmen showed up to his doorstep he was going to put at least a few of those motherfuckers in the dirt. That's what all the guns were for.

When my momma was nine years old the Fieldses' family home burned to the ground following an electrical fire. The incident initiated their move to Clarksdale, where Rosie Lee's parents—my great-grandparents, Claude and Amy McAfee—took them into their home on Barnes Avenue until my grandparents got back on their feet.

My granddaddy hadn't made it past the eighth grade but he didn't allow that to limit him. He was in constant search of the next bigger and better opportunity to provide for his growing family. He didn't need a formal education to see that sharecropping as an American institution was dying off. Mechanical cotton pickers were taking over the work that once required black plantation hands. So he retired from his days as a tenant farmer and took a job at a meat-packing business in Clarksdale called Delta Packing Company.

He worked there for a few years and then got a job in the oil mill which paid a little bit more. This allowed him to move his family out of his in-laws' home and buy a house of their own down the street for $3,000. But Rosie Lee was keeping the kids coming, so it wasn't long before the oil mill wasn't paying enough either. The Fields family was going to need a bigger house.

That's when my granddaddy started making the hour-and-a-half drive up Highway 61 to go to work in Memphis, Tennessee. There he became a driver, then a mechanic at the Campbell Trucking Company. He rose up the ranks, eventually becoming their first black supervisor. A guinea pig for the company's first attempts at racial integration.

He'd spend the week in Memphis and then come back to Clarksdale on the weekends. My momma wouldn't leave his side. On Saturdays he worked on neighbors' cars to bring in a little extra money and she would be outside with him all day, fetching him whatever tools he needed and bringing him something cold to drink to fight off the humid Mississippi heat. The weekends were their time to bond and catch up. My momma was somewhat reserved and shy but she told her daddy any and every thought that crossed her mind. He was her best friend. She didn't open up to anyone else that way, even her momma and younger siblings.

In 1967 my granddaddy purchased an eleven-room brick home from a minister at 428 McKinley Street, a property that is family-owned to this day. They kept the house on Barnes Street and converted it into a small café. The café became Rosie Lee's hustle. She'd work the evening times, when folks would be getting off work and looking for someplace to have a hamburger, drink a beer or a pint of corn whiskey, and dance to music booming from the Seeburg jukebox player.

After graduating high school in 1968 my momma attended Coahoma Junior College for a year before transferring to Mississippi Valley State University, a black college in Leflore County. As focused and disciplined as she was plain old bright, she graduated from the school's nursing program in 1971. It would be the first of several degrees she would earn in the field of health sciences.

Mississippi Valley State is also where my momma encountered my father. He wasn't from the Delta. Born September 26, 1935, William Leonard Roberts was raised in Lloyd, a country town in North Florida situated between Jefferson and Leon County. He was the firstborn son of William Roberts and Mabel Leonard Roberts. Mabel already had a son from a first marriage, my uncle, May Williams. A few years after my father was born they had two more children, my aunt Carrie and my uncle Arthur. We call him Uncle Tudor.

In 1946 the Robertses moved from Lloyd to central Florida, where they settled in a mining community in Polk County called Brewster. Brewster's not around anymore. It's been a ghost town since the sixties. But back then it was a money-making company town for American Cyanamid, whose principal product was phosphate. My granddaddy got a job in the phosphate mines and worked there for nearly forty years until he retired.

Like my granddaddy on my momma's side, William Roberts was not an educated man. But he made sure his children were. He saw that men who worked in the mines were coming out of there with all sorts of cancers—leukemia, lymphoma, mesothelioma—and he wanted his kids to have the options he hadn't. Getting an education was the way out of this radiation-contaminated town.

At home my daddy went by the nickname "Tut," but at school

and throughout the community he was known as "Big Brewster." Everybody knew Big Brewster the Bruiser. He was the star defensive tackle for Union Academy's football team and a standout on the school's wrestling team. The man was a stud. My momma says my daddy and I have the same build. My sister swears we walk the same way.

After graduating from Union Academy in 1956 my father briefly attended Wiley College, a black school in Marshall, Texas. But his studies would be put on hiatus. After his first semester he got drafted into the United States Army. He got deployed to Germany, where he spent his first tour of duty working on a helicopter crew patrolling the Russian border. Upon his return he resumed his education at Florida A&M University in Tallahassee. But he was still in the reserves and after a year at A&M they sent him back to Europe.

Somehow he ended up in New York City following his years in the service. He spent his young adulthood there working as a computer programmer at IBM and later at Chemical Bank. My daddy was a highly intelligent individual, especially when it came to computers.

He finally earned his bachelor's degree in business administration from Delaware State University in 1969. And that's when he headed off to Mississippi Valley State, where he'd accepted a job to become the school's assistant union director.

My daddy had been something of a hometown hero growing up. He was a popular guy who liked to have himself a good time and he most definitely had an eye for the young coeds on Mississippi Valley State's campus. But when he pulled up on my momma in his beige Buick Riviera and tried to talk to her she wasn't going for it. He *was* her type—smart, charming, athletic—but she wasn't interested in dating someone fifteen years her senior, especially an employee at the school. That was frowned upon. Plus she had a boyfriend at the time. A guy on the school's football team named Nathaniel Dorsey, who went on to play for the Pittsburgh Steelers.

My daddy must have figured if this girl had a thing for jocks then eventually he would get his chance. It took him longer than he expected but he finally wore her down. My momma had graduated and was working as a nurse at Taborian Hospital in Mound Bayou. My father had also left Mississippi Valley State and was teaching at Coahoma Community College in Clarksdale while he worked on getting his MBA at Delta State University. But they ran in similar social circles and would see each other out. She had his phone number, and one night when she needed a ride home from work she gave him a call.

One thing led to another that night and soon my momma had a difficult decision to make. She still had feelings for Nathaniel. But she'd long ago made a promise to herself that she would be a virgin for her husband. At the end of the day she couldn't bring herself to break that vow. She ended things with Nathaniel and started going steady with my daddy. Truth be told, I think my momma still wonders about what could have been with that other guy.

My parents got married shortly thereafter at the Coahoma County courthouse and a year and a half later my sister was born. Her name is Tawanda Roberts, but within the family she's known by her middle name. Renee.

My family's decision to move to Miami came about when my father accepted a position to become the business manager at Florida Memorial College in Miami Gardens. My momma had gotten pregnant again so it wasn't the worst time for her to be between jobs. With her nursing background she knew she'd be able to find work and advance her career in Miami.

But she had never lived in a big city like my father had and Miami was a big change. She kept her feelings to herself, but the move wasn't easy on her. This was a country girl from Clarksdale, where there was a clear separation between classes and cultures. She'd spent the first twenty-five years of her life in a tight-knit community with neighbors who had lived next door to each other for generations and looked out for each other. She'd only ever really been around other Southern black folks and all of a sudden she was in this melting pot of Cubans, Haitians, Jamaicans, Bahamians, East Indians and Trinidadians. Her new neighbors practiced Haitian voodoo and Santeria. They would bring home goats to sacrifice in the backyard and smear themselves with the blood after they cut their heads off.

She dealt with all types of culture shock. Driving in Miami was totally overwhelming to her. No one had ever taught her that avenues run from north to south and streets from east to west. She avoided the expressway completely. She became agoraphobic and made few new friends. The local news disturbed her, and she started praying a lot more. These were some of the reasons my momma decided to go back home the week before I was born.

Both of my parents had aspirations that went beyond the simple pleasures of country life in Mississippi. They knew there would be bigger and better opportunities in Miami. For themselves and for their children. What they didn't know was that they were arriving on the precipice of a very bloody and ugly time in the city's history. A storm was coming in. A lot of shit was about to go down.

CHAPTER

2

An epidemic of violent crime, a plague of illicit drugs and a tidal wave of refugees have slammed into South Florida with the destructive power of a hurricane.

—*TIME Magazine* (November 1981)

THE FIRST YEAR OF MY LIFE WAS SPENT IN a house my parents rented in Hialeah, west of Miami. But I don't remember a thing about that place. My earliest memories are in Carol City, at the corner of 183rd Street and 39th Court, where my folks bought a small three-bedroom, two-bathroom home in the spring of 1977.

Aside from its seafoam-green paint job, my house looked like every other one on the block. Due to the hurricanes all of inner city Miami's homes are built the same: concrete, reinforced steel bars and stormproof windows. Inside the house everything was concrete too. The ceiling. The walls. The floors. South Florida is too hot for carpet.

Behind my house was a set of housing projects. In the bushes that separated my backyard and the apartments lived two junkies. Sometimes I'd watch them from my bedroom window. At night I could only make out the flicker of flame from when they'd light up their crack. The cloud of smoke looked different than when my daddy smoked his cigarettes. He smoked Benson & Hedges Menthol 100's. The crack smoke was thicker. It almost looked blue.

One day my curiosity got the better of me and I decided to get a closer look at the dope fiends' doghouse. I crawled through the bushes into their makeshift dwelling and stared at all the straight shooters, empty baggies and cans of Schlitz malt liquor strewn about the space. I couldn't believe there were people who lived like this.

Over the course of the seventies Miami's identity had transformed from a quiet vacation destination and retiree town to the cocaine capital of America. Yayo had become the glamour drug of the rich and famous and nowhere was the American appetite for powder greater than in Miami.

As the blow business exploded, the competing factions of Colombians and Cubans started beefing. After a deadly shootout in broad daylight at the Dadeland Mall on July 11, 1979, the era of the "Cocaine Cowboys" was on and popping. Bodies started dropping every day. The killings blew the lid off the narco underworld that had seized control of the city.

Things were no better on the other side of the law. Six months after the Dadeland shooting five white Miami-Dade police officers were charged with beating a thirty-three-year-old black man to death in Liberty City. His name was Arthur McDuffie.

On the night of December 21, 1979, McDuffie, an insurance salesman and former United States Marine, ran a red light while riding a Kawasaki 900 motorcycle. When the police put on their sirens he took them on a high-speed chase. It would last eight minutes before McDuffie finally gave up, pulling over at the corner of North Miami Avenue and 38th Street. His surrender bought him no mercy. He was swarmed by police, who proceeded to bash his brains in with their nightsticks. The crackers split his skull open "like an egg," the prosecutor later described. McDuffie died from his injuries four days later.

To cover up their crime the police ran over McDuffie's bike and shattered its glass gauges to make it look like his death had come from a traffic accident. It didn't take long for the county medical examiner to keep it real and call bullshit on that.

When the cover-up didn't hold up and five officers were charged, their defense attorneys got the trial moved out of Miami to Tampa, where they secured an all-white jury. Lenore C. Nesbitt, the Miami-Dade circuit judge who gave the green light to move the trial, called the McDuffie case a "time bomb" when asked to explain her decision.

"I don't want to see it go off in my courtroom or in this community," she said.

The trial lasted over a month, but it only took the jury two and a half hours to acquit the police on all charges. In a city with a long history of racial tensions—particularly when it came to black folks' distrust of law enforcement and the criminal justice system—it was the straw that broke the camel's back. The verdict detonated Miami.

The judge had been correct in her assessment of the case but she was wrong to think she could defuse this bomb. It wouldn't matter where this miscarriage of justice took place. Consumed with rage, black Miami residents took to the streets. By sundown their protests had turned into something uglier. Looting and rioting.

For four days inner city Miami burned. By the time it was over eighteen men and women had been killed and hundreds injured. The city suffered $100 million in property damage, all of it in its black communities.

Even though the riots didn't reach Carol City, the McDuffie case still hit home. I was only four at the time so I don't have the

clearest memories from when it all went down. But the riots—
and the ones that took place in Overtown years later—informed
the way I came to understand the world around me. For black
people in Miami, it became a part of our psyche. People talked
about it all the time. Even when they weren't talking about it,
it was hanging in the air.

The race riots happened at the height of the Mariel boatlift,
when Fidel Castro announced that anyone who wanted to leave
Cuba was welcome to. In the six months that followed, Miami
saw the arrival of more than 125,000 Cuban immigrants, 85,000
of whom arrived the same month of the riots. The flood of Cubans coincided with another wave of Haitian immigration in
Miami. The Haitians had been landing in bigger and bigger
numbers throughout the seventies.

In the aftermath of the riots the feeling among a lot of blacks
in Miami was that the refugees made things worse. While we
struggled to find funding to rebuild our broken communities
the Cubans quickly became a powerful force in Miami. They
were getting the lion's share of small business loans backed by
the federal government.

And while the anticommunist Cubans were welcomed with
open arms and granted refugee status, the Haitian "boat people"
and other Afro-Caribbean immigrants were sent to the Krome
Detention Center and were ineligible for the federal aid avail-
able to political refugees. That led to more resentment. While
there was most definitely tension between American blacks and
Haitians, the preferential treatment the Cubans received felt like
another slap in the face to black people.

But my parents didn't raise me to have hate in my heart and I
was still too young to be tripping over any race shit. One of my
good friends was a Chico named Raul. His mother was from
Honduras and his father was a Cuban. We called him White Boy.

Between the drugs, the riots and the flood of immigrants,

there was so much going on. All eyes were on Miami. This was the era that inspired *Scarface* and *Miami Vice*. But to me it all felt normal. It was my baseline. I didn't know anything else.

In the midst of the chaos that surrounded us, inside 18301 Northwest 39th Court was a loving home. Between my momma's work and studies—she'd gone back to school to become a pediatric nurse practitioner—she was a busy lady. But she still found time to cook us up a four-course meal every night. She made all types of quality home cooking—pot roast, meatloaf, baked chicken, fried chicken, liver—with some cornbread and greens on the side and a dessert to top it all off. My momma makes a serious strawberry shortcake.

My sister and I used to fight over control of the television in our den. When we were real young all Renee wanted to watch were the Hanna-Barbera shows: *The Smurfs* and *The Jetsons* and *Scooby-Doo*. Once she got a little bit older she moved on to the black sitcoms of the era: *The Jeffersons* and *The Cosby Show*.

I wanted to play video games. That was my main thing then. Being the computer nerd that he was, my daddy indulged me in my hobby. He let me get all the consoles. He had his Commodore 64 home computer and I had my Atari 2600. Then I got the ColecoVision, which was followed by Neo-Geo and eventually the Nintendo and Super Nintendo.

At some point Renee got a TV in her bedroom so those fights ended. My sister and I have always been extremely close. Renee's a G. We are cut from the same fabric in many ways. All of the older street niggas I became close with later in life. Niggas like Kane, Black, Short Legs, Earl, Wayne, even E-Class were friends with my sister first.

Music always had a presence in our household and could be heard coming from my parents' old-school wooden stereo console, which had an eight-track, record player and radio. Because of my parents' age difference, I was exposed to different generations and genres of music. My daddy played a lot of jazz. Miles Davis, Charlie Parker, Dizzy Gillespie and all the John Coltrane vinyls. My mama was more into soul music and R&B. The Isley Brothers, Isaac Hayes, Bobby Womack, Curtis Mayfield, Tyrone Davis and of course her fellow Clarksdale native Sam Cooke. She loved gospel music too. Mighty Clouds of Joy. The Williams Brothers. Mahalia Jackson. Reverend James Cleveland.

My introduction to hip-hop came at school. I was in the third grade when Luther "Uncle Luke" Campbell and 2 Live Crew released *The 2 Live Crew Is What We Are*, the debut album that took Miami bass music from the city's underground clubs to the mainstream. Out of nowhere, it seemed, Luke's nasty lyrics were booming through the halls of my Miami Gardens Elementary School.

"HEY-Y-Y-Y-Y WE WANT SOME PU-U-USSAY-Y-Y!"

For a third grader, talking about some pussy was just about the rawest shit you could do. I was something of a class clown so it didn't take long before I was singing it in the cafeteria.

Those types of antics eventually got me pulled out of school. When I was in fourth grade I had a young white male instructor. His name was John Gay. Anytime he would try to get me to pay attention in class I would fuck with him.

"You can't tell me what to do. You're Gay."

I thought I could get away with saying that because it was true. The man really was John Gay. But the technicality didn't save me and my momma had to come in to meet with him. He told her my poor grades were a result of my behavior inside the classroom and me not taking school seriously. He was probably right but my momma told him he didn't know how to connect with black boys and she pulled me out of school that day and enrolled me in St. Monica Catholic School.

But when I kept bringing home Ds from private school she brought me back to Miami Gardens Elementary and begged my principal, Mr. Leon, to let me come back. My momma wasn't about to be paying $200 a month for me to be bringing home the same exact grades.

"Will, I can't be coming here every other day," she told me. "I have to work."

I made sure she wouldn't have to. From that day forward I did enough to get by. I'd given up on the idea of being a good student but I did care about not being a burden. I knew my momma was telling the truth when she said she didn't have time for my bullshit. Monday through Friday she worked nine-to-five as a nursing director at Landmark Health Center. On the weekend she worked per diem at Miami General Hospital. On top of that she worked ten hours a week as a nurse consultant.

For a while my daddy worked a lot too. He taught accounting at Miami Dade Community College and he was co-owner of a real estate business that had a subcontract with HUD. If someone defaulted on their mortgage and a house went into foreclosure, his business would board up the house, cut the grass and keep up the property.

But as my father was coming up on his tenth year of teaching at Miami Dade Community College he got laid off. In the state of Florida, you are vested with pension after ten years of service. But if they can find a reason to get rid of you before then, you lose your pension benefits. They were doing a lot of people dirty like that then and that's what happened to him.

Renovatin' the ghettos, movin' me elsewhere
Daddy didn't see pension, they took his healthcare
Affordable housing and they fed us welfare
Showed us Tony Montana, teachers couldn't care less

—"Game Ain't Based on Sympathy,"
Rather You than Me (2017)

My father could have accomplished anything he wanted in this world. The man was damn near a genius. I never once asked him a question he didn't know the answer to. But after they took his pension I think he lost his drive. He started spending a lot more time drinking beers with his buddies outside the corner store.

He still worked. He got a job teaching night classes at Florida International University and did people's income tax on the side. But he just wasn't a hustler the same way my momma was. Like my grandfather, she was always on the hunt for the next thing, whether it be a promotion, another degree, or an extra shift at the hospital. As I got older and my awareness of those things came into focus, I realized my momma was the breadwinner of our household.

2 Live Crew had made me aware of hip-hop but I didn't have anyone to tell me where to take my interest from there. My momma wasn't too fond of cussing, and she was even less fond of the type of foul shit that Luke was talking about.

It wasn't until Jabbar put me onto Too Short that my passion for hip-hop really started to take root. Jabbar was my best friend growing up. He still is. He stayed three houses down and he and I have been down since day one.

Unlike me, Jabbar had a bunch of older brothers and cousins in the neighborhood who were putting him onto all the music that was coming out. We were walking over to the park one day when he passed me the headphones to his Sony Walkman.

"Fatboy, check this out," he told me.

Ronald Reagan came up to me and said, "Do you have the answer?
To the US economy and a cure for cancer?"
I said, "What are you doing in the White House if you're not selling cocaine?

Ask your wife, Nancy Reagan, I know she'll spit that game
Like one night, she came to my house and gave me a blow job
She licked my dick up and down like it was corn on the cob."

—Too Short, "CussWords,"
Life Is…Too Short (1988)

"Yo! Who the fuck is that?!" I asked.

"Too Short," he told me. "He's from Oakland."

This was the moment that hip-hop had my full attention. I needed to know everything there was to know about it.

I started using my lunch money to buy records at the Carol Mart, the flea market on 183rd Street and 27th Avenue. I still didn't know what I should be listening to, so at first I would buy records based on whether or not I liked the cover art. That's how Run-DMC's "Walk This Way" became my first piece of vinyl. I didn't even like the song that much but that cover was cold.

I'd bring my records home and examine their every detail. When I bought *The 2 Live Crew Is What We Are* I liked that the Jeep Cherokee they were riding in had "Luke Skywalker" written across it. I would look out for that Jeep whenever I was riding around the city in the back seat of my momma's car. I thought it was cool that they shot the cover in the alley behind the Pac Jam. It blew my mind when I saw the record had been pressed up in the heart of Liberty City. I knew where those places were.

The first beat I ever wrote a rap to was Rebbie Jackson's 1984 single "Centipede." It was one of my momma's records and the B-side had the song's instrumental. I'd listen to it for hours, jotting down whatever rhymes I could come up with. I wrote to that one beat for months, experimenting with different rhyme patterns and figuring out how to switch up my flow when it switched up.

Miss Nelly, my music teacher at Miami Gardens Elementary, encouraged me to start writing raps with a theme instead of just focusing on making them rhyme. I took heed of her instructions, and me and my homie Bishop came up with a song called "Where the Hoes at?"

"Where the Hoes at?" was a song about the baddest bitches at Miami's five main black high schools: Norland, Jackson, Northwestern, Central and Carol City High. Each verse corresponded with a different school and day of the week. I kicked the song off with Monday and Tuesday and then Bishop and his older brother handled Wednesday through Friday.

It's Monday morning, there was nothing to do
I was cruising with the homies, chilling with my crew
We had this feeling, to rush some hoes
There was nothing stopping us, we had 30s and lows
At the red light we all made our plan
We wanted some hoes, so we went to Norland
By this time it's lunch hour so we went to the trucks
There were hoes for everyone so we were all in luck
I rushed more and more, I rushed three and four
And you know they went crazy when I bust through the door
Cause I'm a dog in heat, that's the game I play
Hoes was marching to the Chevy like it was a parade
I had a day of pleasure, that's how it goes
That's my point of view, Norland got them hoes

It's Tuesday, I was looking for action
So I made a little stop at a school called Jackson
As I turned around the corner, what did I see?
A posse of hoes walking straight towards me!
I was dressed to impress, I was feeling proud

So you know I had to rush the baddest girl in the crowd
This girl was a problem, she wouldn't leave me alone
24/7 just ringing my phone
School's okay, the girls don't play
And I had to thank everyone for the fun I had today
Cause I'm a female pleaser, that's how it goes
That's my point of view, Jackson got them hoes

—"Where the Hoes at?" (1986)

Miss Nelly was not the biggest fan of the subject matter of "Where the Hoes at?" but she loved that Bishop and I had taken our assignment seriously. She arranged for us to perform the song at a "Just Say No to Drugs" event at Carol City Park. That was the first time I ever took the stage.

Bishop and I were certain we had a hit record on our hands. We hopped on our bikes and rode from Carol City all the way to Miami Lakes. That's where Uncle Luke stayed. Luke had a big-ass crib on the golf course and we knew if we could catch him coming out his house and perform this song for him, we were going to be millionaires. There was no doubt in our minds.

We couldn't find Luke and "Where the Hoes at?" never did become the breakout hit Bishop and I expected it to be. But the feedback and encouragement I'd gotten from Miss Nelly and the response from the crowd at Carol City Park planted a seed in my mind. Rapping was something I was good at.

Hip-hop would also introduce me to the world that existed outside Miami. I started discovering guys like Eric B and Rakim, Big Daddy Kane, N.W.A. and the Geto Boys. I'd never been to places like New York or Los Angeles or Houston but when I closed my eyes and listened to the music it transported me to the different worlds these guys were coming from. I'd never met an Asian person in my life but when Ice Cube rapped about the racist Korean store owners harassing niggas out in LA, I could see myself standing outside the store with a forty-ounce in my hand. My records became my passport stamps.

Everything about the culture fascinated me. I lined the walls of my bedroom with posters of LL Cool J, Big Daddy Kane, EPMD, Salt-N-Pepa, Special Ed and MC Shan that I pulled out of *Word Up!* and *Right On!* magazine. I watched movies like *Beat Street* and *Breakin'* and learned the four elements of hip-hop— DJing, MCing, B-Boying and graffiti. I was obsessed with the fashion too. The Dapper Dan pieces Eric B. and Rakim wore on the cover of *Paid in Full.* The Cazal shades that Run-DMC were rocking. Slick Rick's eye patch and the gold ropes he had around his neck. A rapper from Philadelphia I liked named Cool C wore a red silk sweat suit and red suede low-top Bally sneakers with the holes in them. Only the dope boys in Miami wore Ballys.

I remember being in the arcade at the Carol Mart one day and seeing the music video for Marley Marl and the Juice Crew's "The Symphony" playing on the big screen. There was a group of girls there and the baddest one out of all of them started talking about how fine she thought Big Daddy Kane was. Her mouth was damn near watering. I started growing out my flat-top that day.

Soon my lunch money and the couple dollars I'd make cutting neighbors' grass and carrying old Spanish ladies' groceries to their car wasn't enough to keep up with the pace at which my record collection was expanding. So when I was thirteen I got a job at the car wash on the corner of 183rd Street and 27th Avenue.

On weekends I'd be there from 8:00 a.m. to 8:00 p.m. A day's work was $30 plus tips. I made sure I got me some tips. When the dope boys would pull in they'd get the first class treatment. I'd wash their car, vacuum the interior and degrease the seats if needed. Before I finished I'd go through their cassettes to see what they were listening to. Then I'd organize them in alphabetical order. It wasn't long before all the hustlers were requesting "Windex William," the dirty little fat nigga, to service their cars.

Hip-hop was no longer just a hobby. It became an all-consuming obsession. The way that I took to rapping...it was the closest thing to what I imagined those junkies behind my house felt when that crack smoke hit their lips.

CHAPTER

3

THE EIGHTIES GAVE RISE TO A NEW BREED

of kingpin in Miami. Cocaine was no longer just a rich man's drug and crack had infiltrated the inner city. It wasn't the Co-caine Cowboys fighting for control of the drug market anymore. It was the urban dope boys. Ghetto superstars and hood legends like Isaac "Big Ike" Hicks, Rick "The Mayor" Brownlee, Bo Diddley, Bunkie Brown and Convertible Burt.

Jabbar's daddy was one of these hustlers. Big Mike. Mike was a real Geechi nigga out of Liberty City. He had a curly perm and a mouth full of gold teeth. But hiding behind his Cazal shades were the eyes of a man who was not to be fucked with. Mike was on a level where any number of young shooters would have loved to handle any situation for him but he preferred to do his own dirty work. When I was real young Mike went over to his sister's house after he found out the father of her son was still beating on her. The last time Mike went over there he'd warned this dude to keep his hands off his sister. This time he went to the house and put two shots in his dome. Then he raised his sister's son like he was his own.

Mike was one of the original Miami Boys, a crew that was running boy and girl—heroin and coke—throughout the Southeast United States. We'll get into that more a little bit later because for the first ten years of Jabbar and I's friendship we really didn't get into too much trouble. Most of our time together was spent playing at the park or at each other's houses on some joysticks. We would hitch rides on the back of the ice cream truck and go fishing for bass and brim fish out of the nearby canal. We had to keep an eye out for poisonous water moccasins. So many different creatures inhabit the waters of South Florida.

For a while the baddest shit Jabbar and I did was fistfights. We fought *a lot* as kids. With each other and with other kids at school and in the neighborhood. This was the era when it was all about proving you had hands. Fighting was how you got ranked and respected. The weakest shit you could be was a cur, a dog that don't fight.

A lot of this fighting was orchestrated by Kello, one of the older boys who lived up the street from me. Kello was my official bully growing up. That's putting it nicely. Really Kello was a psychotic menace. He loved to fight and he loved to make other kids fight too. He would plan it out so his most high-profile scraps took place on Friday and Saturday nights at the park when everyone would be there to watch.

Kello's partners in crime were Jon-Jon and his cousin Steve. Jon-Jon lived on my street too and he was pretty sadistic himself. He thought about evil shit. I remember Jon-Jon came to my house one morning and started knocking on the door. I was still in my drawers when I came out to see what he wanted.

"The Devil rode my back... The Devil ain't never rode your back, Fatboy?!"

"Nah...what that feel like?"

"It's like you wake up but you can't move...your eyes are open but your eyes are closed..."

I'm telling you. Something was seriously wrong with these niggas.

Steve was from Overtown but he would take the bus to Carol City to hang with Kello and Jon-Jon. Steve had two gold front teeth embossed with dollar signs, which he'd financed by robbing people. He was planning on robbing his way up to eight. It could be a hundred degrees out and Steve would be in his same black hoodie with a black skully on.

The funny thing is Kello and Jon-Jon were both church boys! Kello would be in church every Sunday with his momma. She was a big black lady who looked like Florida Evans from *Good Times*.

One Sunday Kello had to read Scripture in front of the whole congregation. When he started stuttering over his words I busted out laughing. Jabbar kicked me, knowing that I was going to live to regret that, but it only made me laugh even harder.

Kello stopped reading right in the middle of church to address me in front of everyone.

"Boy oh boy... The things I'm gon' do to you..."

The next day Kello had me come over. One thing about these boys is that if you didn't do what they said, whatever they had in store for you was only going to get worse. Kello was so crazy that if I didn't come over of my own volition he would just sit outside my bedroom window till I came out. So I went over there and had Jabbar come with me. Kello's momma was in the kitchen cooking up some hog maw and collard greens when he brought me into his bedroom and closed the door behind us. That's when he handed me one of his momma's clothespins.

"Take your shirt off," he said. "Put this on your nipple."

"Excuse me?"

"Don't make me swing on you, boy. Just put it on your nipple. Sixty seconds."

For the first fifteen seconds I played it cool. By the half minute mark I had tears streaming down my face. By the time it was over I was certain I had just split my nipple in half. Kello finally took it off and let me go home.

But I loved Kello! All his bullying came out of a place of love and it toughened me and Jabbar up. When it came to fighting anyone in our own age bracket we were so far advanced because we'd grown up fighting these older niggas who were specialists with their hands.

That was pretty much the extent of my bullying growing up. It wasn't until me and Jabbar started riding our bikes over to Miss Angel's apartment that things turned a corner. That's when everything changed from the typical boyhood mischief of two jits coming up in Carol City into something more sinister. I was only twelve but very quickly I was exposed to a level of criminal activity that most grown men never see.

Miss Angel was Jabbar's auntie and she stayed in the Matchbox. The Matchbox was a beige two-story walk-up apartment complex at the intersection of 199th Street and 37th Avenue and it was known as the home of the Carol City crackhead. As far as projects go, it was not a very big one, but when it came to selling dope, the place was on fire. That's why they called it the Matchbox.

The front section of the Matchbox was run by Fat Sean. Sean was a wild, junkyard dog type of nigga. He had a big beard and a whole mop of hair on his head, which was never combed or brushed. It was good hair though. Looking at Sean you might mistake him for a Chico. He would be posted outside his spot, rolling dice or arguing with his bitch and he'd have a couple kilos inside—hard and soft—ready to serve.

Canhead controlled the back of the Matchbox. Canhead was

a short, light-skinned nigga with freckles and sandy red hair.
I didn't interact with him too much but he was a cool nigga.
He wasn't a brute like Sean was. Canhead was a DJ along with
being a hustler and he would set up his turntables and speakers
outside and throw block parties for the Matchbox.

Most of my time at the Matchbox was spent in the middle
section. That's where Miss Angel stayed, and her apartment was
the headquarters of a crew of guys that would soon rule over
Carol City. These guys were all several years older than me and
Jabbar. This is where I became acquainted with guys like Boobie, Graylin, Bernard, Fishgrease, Cat Eye Moses and D-Green.

There was *a lot* of shit going down at Miss Angel's. A table
crew might be set up in the dining room chopping up the dope.
They used cutting agents to stretch the product, dilute its purity
and maximize profits. There might be a nigga in the kitchen
mixing up coke and baking soda in a Pyrex pot. I was at Angel's the first time I saw an ounce of powder get cooked down
straight drop. The crack didn't come back white like the coke.
It had a yellowish hue. Wrapped in plastic the zone looked like
a macadamia nut cookie.

Of those aforementioned hustlers, Kenneth "Boobie" Williams would go on to become the most infamous. When he
landed himself on *America's Most Wanted* a decade later, he would
be introduced to the world as the ringleader of the Boobie Boys,
a vicious street gang behind an $85 million drug ring, thirty-
five murders and more than one hundred shootings.

But when Jabbar and I first started hanging in the Matchbox
there was no such thing as the Boobie Boys. Boobie wasn't even
there in the beginning. He was in Miami-Dade's Juvenile Detention Center, fighting a murder charge from a shooting in River
City in October of 1987 that left one dead and two wounded.

If there was a leader of this crew then it was Graylin. Graylin was only sixteen when I met him but he had the physical-

ity and presence of a grown man. He was the type who would fight ten niggas at the drop of a dime and win. Graylin was a cold-blooded, aggressive motherfucker. His nickname was The Grinch.

Graylin was the first dope boy I remember seeing break out the foreign cars. This was the late eighties and it was still the era of candy-painted donks in Miami. Box Chevys and Cadillac Broughams and Fleetwoods sitting on 30s and lows. But sixteen-year-old Graylin pulled up one day in a brand-new white BMW convertible. I remember he put a dollar food stamp behind the glass of the frame of his license plate. So that he never forgot where he came from. I thought that was the flyest shit ever.

Graylin's Beamer was impressive but it was his penchant for violence that left a lasting impression on me. There was one incident in particular. Soon after I started hanging in the Matchbox, Graylin began messing with a stripper named Pinky. *Everybody* from Miami knows Pinky. She was considered to be one of the baddest bitches in Dade County.

This put Graylin at odds with a jealous ex-boyfriend of Pinky's, who happened to be one of the most feared gangsters in Liberty City. He was a big dog in the 22nd Avenue Gang. Now I don't know all the specifics as to how this beef over a hoe unfolded, but I do know how it ended. Graylin pulled up on this dude outside of a soul food restaurant in Liberty City called Jumbo's and blew his brains out. He just rolled up on him in his drop top and opened fire. The end.

When the streets got to talking about what had happened I couldn't believe it. I knew Graylin was cutthroat. His reputation preceded him. But the other dude was supposed to be on a whole different level. He was in his thirties and had been in the streets for decades, and this teenager had just come and knocked him off like it was nothing. It seemed impossible. The incident left an everlasting impression on me. I knew then that any nigga could get it and that any nigga could give it. That nobody was exempt.

I wouldn't see Graylin for a long time after that. He went on the run for a few months until the feds caught him trapping up in Tallahassee. He got twelve years for that but he allegedly almost caught a triple murder while he was awaiting the outcome of the case. The rumor was Graylin beat three other inmates to death with his bare hands at the USP in Atlanta. He got cleared of those charges on account of self-defense but he wouldn't get so lucky when it came to the murder charges he was facing back home. He pled guilty and received a fifteen-year sentence.

Right around the time that Graylin went in, his best friend Boobie was coming home. Boobie had pled guilty to attempted second-degree murder from the shooting in River City and served a couple years in juvie. When he got home he quietly became the leader of the Matchbox.

Graylin was a leader people feared. He commanded respect by way of force. Boobie was different. He didn't drink, smoke or even use profane language. His leadership was rooted in finesse. He was a person who people genuinely liked and wanted to be associated with. Now don't get it fucked up, Boobie was by far the most on go nigga in the history of Carol City. He did not hesitate to drop the hammer when a situation called for it and he felt like the situation called for it a lot. But it just wasn't his first instinct like it was Graylin's. There was a difference. He was more cerebral in his decision-making. Everything was calculated. Unlike Graylin, Boobie had this way of masking his iron fist by slipping it into a velvet glove.

Prison can be like college for a young criminal mind. During his stint, Boobie built relationships with dope boys from all over Dade County. Niggas from Liberty City, Overtown, Brownsville, Opa-locka, Little River and Little Haiti. When he came home those connections grew into a network of like-minded hustlers. That was how Boobie started building an empire.

Niggas like Fat Sean and Canhead had no aspirations beyond running their little traps in Carol City, nor did they have the capacity to do so. But even as he ascended to kingpin, Boobie always carried himself more like an ambassador than a dictator. His vision extended beyond the Matchbox.

Miss Angel's apartment wasn't just a drug lab. It was an armory where everybody stashed their guns. It was a safe house to lay low at following home invasions. Because as much as Boobie and his crew were dope boys, they were robbers too. They had a serious stick-up operation going. If one of them got tipped off about a nearby stash house holding bricks they would ski-mask up and go take them.

They were hitting the pawn shops and department stores too. Miami is where smash-and-grab burglaries were invented. They'd round up a few stolen cars and drive one straight through the stores' front windows. They'd load up the others with as much jewelry, guns and clothes as they could and take off into the night.

Jabbar and I were sleeping over Miss Angel's the first time I saw them come back from one of these excursions. It was the middle of the night when they busted in, fussing and fighting over the spoils and who was getting what. Whatever clothes didn't fit them or little chains they decided they didn't want, they let me and Jabbar have. We looked up to these niggas and they looked out for us. At first they probably tolerated us because they knew and respected Big Mike, but eventually they took a genuine liking to us.

T-Man and Triece were the first niggas to front me and Jabbar ounces of crack. We were so young we really didn't know what to do with it. We just knew we wanted in. So we brought it to Angel's son, Jabbar's cousin Arthur, who showed us how to cut it up into different size rocks and explained to us our profit margins.

We eventually realized that Arthur was robbing us. Since he actually lived at Miss Angel's he knew where we hid our bomb and when Jabbar and I would go home for the night he would go cut up a bunch of rocks for himself out of our stash. It was all love though. Getting finessed was one of the growing pains of learning the dope game.

These guys knew we were too little to be taking over other niggas' corners so they let us get off our little sacks out of Miss Angel's. When a junkie would come in looking for something small to get him 'til the next day, they'd send them our way to put a couple dollars in our pockets. They looked out for us.

When I look back on the path I started heading down I can't say I didn't know any better. My family was by no means rich but we weren't living in roach-infested projects either. Carol City was considered a middle-class neighborhood. It was a refuge from the violence that was happening in Liberty City and Overtown.

I'd come from a household with two educated and successful parents. I couldn't blame them. Nobody was smoking crack. Nobody was beating on each other. My daddy smoked too many cigarettes and drank too many Michelob Ultras but it wasn't like his vices were tearing our house apart. He was always real smooth with it.

But around the time I started hanging out in the Matchbox my life at home changed. When I was eleven my parents told my sister and I they were separating. Over the years they had grown to love and respect one another and they'd made a loving home for their children. But I don't know if my parents were ever in love in *that way*. They didn't have that type of affectionate relationship.

As far as divorces go it wasn't a nasty one. There was no talking bad about each other or fighting over money or the house. There were no lawyers involved. They handled it well. But my daddy moved back up to North Florida and I didn't see him too much after that.

> My daddy caught a bus, never looking back
> Got me standing in the rain, first 50 pack

—"Fascinated,"
Port of Miami 2 (2019)

My father's absence left a void at home. My momma started having to work even more than she already was and I started spending more time with guys like Boobie and Big Mike. The dope boys became my role model figures.

The way the feds tell it, Boobie and Mike were monsters preying on their own kind. But I saw a different side of that story. Every Christmas, Boobie would host a toy drive at the Omega Center where hundreds of toys would be given out to the youth of Carol City.

So to me they were Robin Hood types. All the "Just Say No to Drugs" messaging I was getting at school was telling me the dope was ruining a lot of lives. But at the same time I was seeing smiles on kids' faces when they got their first bikes for Christmas. The ethics of hustling was complicated. The line between right and wrong was fuzzy.

When I first started elementary school I wanted to be a good student. Both of my parents were smart as hell and I looked up to them. But as the years went on I started realizing that I was damn near retarded when it came to school. Do you know how badly I would have liked to learn Spanish? The prettiest girl in my school was Puerto Rican and she was my first love. Once a week she'd come to class in her favorite Menudo T-shirt. That was the boy band all the Spanish girls liked back then. I would have loved to be able to say some fly Papi Chulo shit to her.

Math was the worst. When it came time to learn the multiplication tables I had some sort of mental block. My momma got me the flash cards. She hired a tutor for me at one point. I just could not memorize those. That was really the reason I became the class clown. It was the one thing in school I got positive feedback from.

But for some reason when Arthur showed me and Jabbar how to bust down an ounce, that was something I could wrap my head around. Twenty-eight grams in an ounce. Thirty-six ounces in a kilo. If I sell a gram for $50…it made sense to me.

Big Mike tried to keep us out the streets at first. He didn't like that Jabbar and I were hanging out in the Matchbox. He knew what was going on at Angel's and didn't want us to be a part of it. He'd sent Jabbar to Our Lady of Perpetual Help—the Catholic school in Opa-locka that all the dope boys' kids went to—and eventually he took him out of Miami altogether.

The problem was Mike never shielded us from seeing all the money. Or his gold 500 SEL Benz with the champagne leather seats and windshield wipers on the headlights. Or the bricks wrapped in cellophane. Or his .308 Winchester with the bubble level scope. You could hit a nigga in another city with that rifle.

See, it's one thing to tell a couple jits that selling drugs is wrong. But when you show them what a million dollars looks like and have them count it for you, that message goes in one ear and out the other. Suddenly Old Scrappy—that's what we called my daddy's Buick—didn't seem like a nice enough car for me. Suddenly working 8:00 a.m. to 8:00 p.m. at the car wash and staying on the straight and narrow didn't seem all that appealing either. But Mike did try to warn us.

"Only one out of a thousand hustlers make it," Mike would always say. "When you get older you're either going to be broke, dead or serving a life sentence. Trust me, those are the only things that are going to happen."

It was too late though. I had already seen too much. I was infatuated with wealth. I was infected with greed.

CHAPTER

4

FOOTBALL HAS ALWAYS BEEN BIG IN FLOR-
ida, but when I was growing up it was really the shit. I was seven
when the Miami Dolphins picked Dan Marino in the 1983 NFL
Draft. There wasn't too much hype about Marino at first. John
Elway was most definitely the crown jewel of that draft class.
But that changed as soon as Marino got his first snap. Overnight
he became the face of the franchise.

The 1983 football season was also when the University of
Miami won its first national championship, upsetting the top-
ranked University of Nebraska Cornhuskers at the Orange Bowl.
The Hurricanes would go on to add three more titles in '87, '89
and '91, solidifying a legacy as one of the greatest college football dynasties of all time.

It wasn't always that way. For years the U's football program
had been an embarrassment and the school was close to shutting
it down. In a last-ditch effort to turn things around the adminis-

tration hired Howard Schnellenberger to be head coach in 1979. Schnellenberger had been the offensive coordinator under Don Shula when the Dolphins went undefeated in 1972.

Schnellenberger really shook the whole operation up. Even after he left the U following that first championship, the impact he made on the school and the city lived on.

We loved those Hurricanes teams because they were home-grown. Schnellenberger switched up the whole playbook when it came to scouting and recruiting high school prospects. Instead of chasing the same blue chips every other coach was after, he honed in on the hotbed of overlooked talent that was in his backyard. He started recruiting black boys from all over South Florida to this rich white private school in Coral Gables.

When 2 Live Crew came on the scene they repped hard for the U. They wore Hurricanes Starter jackets on their album cover and Luke was an unofficial booster for the program. The success of the U was something that black Miami could take pride in and feel a part of. In the aftermath of the race riots, football played a big part in the city's healing process.

Statistically the odds of playing Division I football, let alone making it to the league, were slim to none. But I was seeing guys like Melvin Bratton go from the streets of Liberty City to catching passes in the Super Bowl. I was seeing Alonzo High-smith get drafted by the Houston Oilers. I was seeing Richmond Webb, left tackle for the Miami Dolphins, riding around Carol City in his white-on-white Benz. Those stories made it feel attainable. It seemed within reach. These people looked like me. They talked like me. They were only a little bit older than me. Why couldn't it be me?

For starters I was never allowed to play youth football. Pop Warner and the Optimist league had weight limits for its age groups. I never fell within those limits. For a thirteen-year-old the limit was something like 140 pounds. By the time I turned thirteen, I was already well over 200 pounds.

My nickname was "Fatboy" but that was never really a source of shame for me. I wore it like a badge of honor. I looked like my daddy and he'd been a jock, a veteran, an educated businessman and an overall confident person. I inherited his confidence. To this day, the Roberts men carry their weight well. I wouldn't even say we're fat. We're just some burly, handsome niggas who smell good.

I was too fat to play football with my friends and that was not a great feeling. I wanted a trophy. There was a coach who let me practice with his team during the week, but come game day I'd have to watch from the bleachers with all the other spectators. That was a little embarrassing. At one point I bought a sauna suit at The Sports Authority to try and get the weight off. I quickly realized that wasn't happening. I wasn't even close.

Once I got to high school my weight no longer prevented me from playing football. Instead, it became an asset. Alfonzo Morgan was in the same boat as me. I don't remember how big Fonzo was when we first met during tryouts our freshman year but by senior year I was six-foot-two, 292 pounds and he was something like six-foot-five, 330. We were some big boys.

It took a special type of person to coach the Carol City Chiefs. Our team was made up of a bunch of wild niggas. We used to break into our rival schools at night and shatter the trophy cases and spray the fire extinguishers everywhere. We'd vandalize the whole place.

The one man who could keep us under control was Walt "Big Money" Frazier, one of the great high school football coaches in Florida state history. The nickname was a joke. We called Coach Frazier "Big Money" because he wore the same clothes and train conductor hat every day. We never saw him spend a dime. We figured Frazier must have a lot of paper stacked up somewhere.

Frazier taught us the game of football but he taught us more than that. For boys like me and Fonzo—my daddy had moved away and Fonzo's was dead—he was a father figure. He showed us how to become men and instilled in us the value of hard work and discipline.

Frazier ran practice like a drill sergeant and he took the same approach with us off the field. One time Fonzo and I were acting up in English class and our teacher asked him to intervene. He came up to us during practice that afternoon.

"I told Ms. Maniscalco to send you two jackasses to my office the next time y'all want to act up," he started. "When you get there, I'm going to turn over my desk. Then I'm going to break the legs off the table and give them to you...so that you can defend yourself from me."

Frazier wasn't bluffing. The man was fearless. There was one time a shoot-out broke out in the stands during a game against our rivals, Miami Northwestern. Once niggas started shooting everybody hit the deck. Everybody except for Frazier, that is. He didn't even budge.

"Coach, get down!" one of us shouted out. "We need you!"

"I bleed orange and black!" Frazier yelled back.

I wore number sixty-one—a tribute to the highway my granddaddy took from Clarksdale to Memphis to go to work. Once I learned the fundamentals I started running through my opponents. The Chiefs' offensive line was mean as hell and we were hitting so many pancake blocks we became known throughout our conference as the IHOP Boys.

I got pretty good. My senior year I was named All-Dade first team offense by *The Miami Herald*. There were a lot of people who believed I had a bright future as a football player. Coach Frazier. My teammates. My classmates. My momma and sister. I believed in myself too. But I never got the recognition from the person I think I wanted it from most. My father. Our relationship had been at a stalemate since he moved away and it hurt that he never came down for one of my games. I wanted for Big Brewster to see what his boy was doing on the football field.

One thing that I wish I could change
Just to see my daddy wavin' at a football game
Just to see my daddy standin' when they say my name
Walk me to the locker room and say, "Son, good game!"
You make a tackle, but nobody there to clap
So I'm writing down my feelings, never knew it was a rap

—"I'm Only Human,"
Trilla (2008)

As much as I loved playing football, I didn't have the tunnel vision focus and total dedication to the game you need to excel at the highest level. By the time I got to high school I already had several extracurricular activities going on.

I'd graduated from selling nicks and dimes in the Matchbox and was starting to touch some weight. One of my first times doing so came about while I was hanging at Jabbar's house one afternoon and saw Big Mike disposing of several trash bags of weed. Mike was getting a lot of weed from the Bahamas and Jamaica then. He had his own speedboat and would zoom down there and pick up loads himself.

This particular batch had gone bad. The air-conditioning in Mike's house had blown out, running nearly two hundred pounds of it.

"You're really about to throw all that away?" I asked.

"It ain't no good," he said.

"We could put carrots in it," I told him. "I heard carrots preserve weed."

Mike knew where I was going and he wasn't trying to hear any of it. He immediately turned his attention to Jabbar.

"Boy, don't you dare go trying to sell this garbage with this dumb nigga," he said. "He's going to leave the house with a thousand dollars' worth of this bullshit and come back with $995 worth, five dollars in cash, and a lump on his forehead."

I wasn't going to be dissuaded. For Mike, a loss like this was not the end of the world. It was the cost of doing business. But to me that was a lot of money to be tossing in a dumpster. So I climbed in there and took it all out.

It would take a while but me and Jabbar ended up selling every ounce of that rotten weed. We called it "Headbanga Boogie" because smoking that shit would give you a headache. The carrots definitely didn't fix the problem.

More weight meant more money. And more money meant more problems. By ninth grade Jabbar had dropped out of high school and was ten toes deep in the streets. I was still in school and playing football—but I had at least one foot firmly planted in. Things were escalating.

Jabbar was living in a rooming house in Liberty City and had set up shop over there. Eventually the niggas who claimed the area caught wind that someone was short stopping their block. These niggas hustled outside the store up the street and Jabbar was catching their customers before they got there with better dope at better prices. They showed up to Jabbar's spot and told him he had to find somewhere else to sling.

Jabbar did find a different spot. He stopped selling out of the rooming house and moved over to the park. But he must have still been affecting these dudes' pockets because they showed up there and said he couldn't hustle there either.

"We gon' see where I can and can't hustle at, then," Jabbar told them.

At that point Jabbar called me and told me the situation we had on our hands. I picked him up and we drove over to the store these niggas hustled at. I had Jabbar wait in the car while I hollered at the leader of the crew, who had told Jabbar to step down. I let him know that was my brother and any problems he had with him, he had with me too. Things got tense but we got out of there before anything other than words were exchanged.

I must have said something about us claiming Carol City because a couple hours later Boobie was knocking at the door of Jabbar's rooming house.

"What's up with you niggas?"

"Nothing... What happened?"

"You gon' sit here and tell me you two ain't got no problems with these niggas around here?"

"Well, yeah, me and Fatboy—"

"I already know," Boobie said. "Because these niggas were talking about running up in this house and killing y'all."

"So what we fitting to do?"

"Nothing. They heard you were from Carol City so their big homies checked in with me and I told him to give you a pass. But y'all niggas is wild. Jabbar, you're short stopping where you lay your head at. And, Fatboy...you're out here driving your momma's car and pulling up on niggas. Both of y'all need to fucking relax."

This wasn't the first time Boobie had to come to our defense. On another occasion Jabbar and I did a drive-by and sprayed up the block of this guy who had disrespected us. Nobody got hit because we weren't aiming at anyone. We were just trying to send a message not to fuck with us. But the message got a little lost in translation.

The nigga we rolled up on also happened to have problems with Boobie for different reasons. But they thought our drive-by was done on Boobie's behalf. When Boobie found out these niggas were mounting an assault because these two young boys in a gray Cadillac opened fire on them, he came to see us.

"Look, I ain't gonna be taking on all this beef for you niggas if y'all ain't even getting out the car and killing," he told us. "You get out, you walk up on your target, and you shoot, you understand?"

I got arrested for the first time when I was sixteen. Once again I'd taken my momma's Baby Lac out for a spin. Me and Fonzo were on our way to a house party and we stopped at a trap in Opa-locka to get a bag of weed. As soon as we made the hand-to-hand the crackers pulled us over. It was a sting.

The Baby Lac got impounded and Fonzo and I were taken to Opa-locka police lockup, where we were booked on drug and firearm charges. I had a .22 in the car when they pulled us over. After we got photographed and fingerprinted they were fitting to transfer us to Miami-Dade County Jail with the real wolves. We tried telling them we were only sixteen but Fonzo and I were so big they didn't believe us. Luckily my momma arrived at the station before that happened and bailed us out. She got us a lawyer who was able to get the case sealed. That was the first time my momma had an idea that I was getting into some trouble. Even then I played it off pretty good. Fonzo had taken the gun charge and I'd taken the one for drug possession, so she still didn't think I was doing much more than smoking a little weed.

I still received recruitment letters from a handful of Division I and II schools that were interested in having me play football. Florida State University. Colorado State. Clemson. But everybody thought that I was headed to the University of Miami. At school I'd gotten another nickname, "Big East," because it seemed like a foregone conclusion I would be joining the NCAA's Big East Conference.

My momma felt differently. She wasn't too keen on me staying in Miami. Aside from my arrest, I'd done a good job keeping
her in the dark about what I was up to. But she knew I didn't
have to be a dope boy to get killed and that I didn't have to be
a killer to catch a 187. Her fear was that I would get caught up
in something that had nothing to do with me. That I would be
riding in one of my homies' cars when some shit popped off.
Depending on which way it went I could either catch a stray
bullet or a charge of accessory to murder.

My momma also wasn't comfortable with me attending what
she considered a "white school." Our family had a history of attending black colleges. She knew a guy named Wayne Campbell,
who was the assistant football coach at Albany State University,
an HBCU in Georgia. Wayne was able to get the school to offer
me a full ride and he pitched me on the idea of joining Albany
State's Golden Rams football team.

The Rams had won their conference the season prior, and
several former players had gone on to the NFL. Wayne told me
I'd have an opportunity to make a real impact at Albany State
instead of having to ride the bench at one of the bigger D-I
schools. Honestly I can't remember if Wayne sold me on that
or if I just wanted to make my momma happy. One way or another, Albany State is where I decided to go.

When I reported for preseason in the summer of '94, the
school was in rough shape. Tropical Storm Alberto had fucked
up the Southeast United States a few weeks earlier, causing
thirty-two deaths and more than a billion dollars in property
damage. The rainfall was so severe that the Flint River over-
flowed, flooding the city of Albany. The papers were calling it
Georgia's worst natural disaster ever.

It was not a good start to my college experience. Two-thirds
of Albany State's campus was underwater so instead of moving
into dorms we were housed in trailers at a nearby military base.

Without a suitable field to play on, the team spent the first few weeks of preseason helping the Red Cross with their relief efforts. I didn't mind that, but the living situation was a problem. I wasn't touching too much dope at the time but I did keep a pistol in my room and was smoking weed heavy. So I had a bunch of shit that I had no business bringing onto a military base. It was a recipe for catching a case.

As a crab—that's what they call freshman players—I didn't see too many snaps once the season started. But I did like what they were doing with the football program at Albany State. I liked Wayne and the rest of the coaching staff. I liked my teammates. Fonzo ended up transferring to Albany State from a junior college in California and the idea of reuniting the IHOP Boys was appealing.

If playing ball was the only thing I had to do then I may have stayed. But I could not do all the school stuff. I was failing my classes and I had no interest in putting in the work to pass them. My education was the last thing on my mind. I was living the life of a broke college student and all I could think about was how much money I was missing out on by being there.

When I drove out to Grandma's house in Mississippi for Christmas break I told her that I didn't think college was for me.

"But, Will, your mother is a nurse practitioner. Your father is a professor. You need to go to college."

She knew my momma was going to be devastated. My sister had just followed in her footsteps and enrolled in her alma mater, Mississippi Valley State. My uncle Tudor had gone to Tuskegee University and my aunt Carrie had gone to Rutgers. All of my cousins, on both sides of my family, had gone to college. My momma was the one responsible for getting me this full-ride to Albany State and now I wanted to drop out after my first semester.

I did go back after the winter break but I was counting down the days till the end of the school year. I wasn't sure what my future had in store but I knew it wasn't here. I finished out the school year and moved back home.

CHAPTER

5

ONCE I WAS BACK IN MIAMI I WAS BACK AT
the Pac Jam. Located in the heart of Liberty City at 84th Street and
Northeast 2nd Avenue, the Pac Jam Teen Disco was the underage
nightclub owned by Uncle Luke. Whether you were thirteen or
thirty, from Liberty City, Carol City, Overtown or Opa-locka, the
Pac Jam was the place to be on Friday and Saturday nights.

Monday through Friday, the two-story space served as the headquarters of Luke Records. But once the weekend rolled around the
first-floor warehouse would get cleared out and converted into the
Pac Jam. The walls would be lined with speakers and subwoof-
ers stacked on top of each other. Then the Ghetto Style DJs, local
legends like DJ Amazing Chico, would come spin booty-shaking
bass music for more than a thousand Miami teenagers.

Throughout high school I'd been a "Pac Jam Junkie," a title you
could only claim if you were really in there every weekend. Me
and my homies would get fresh beforehand. You might see me in

the Pac Jam in a fresh Tommy Hilfiger polo with a crisp pair of jeans I'd just gotten back from the dry cleaners. We used heavy starch on our jeans to get the good crease. I had the gold Saint Lazarus pendant around my neck, a Figaro bracelet on one wrist and a Guess watch on the other. I didn't have money yet but I had the blueprint of what getting money looked like.

Right around the time I moved back to Miami, Luke hosted a talent show at the Pac Jam where the grand prize was a deal at Luke Records. Pursuing my music seriously had been on my mind since I left school but I wasn't ready to perform at the Pac Jam. It was not the friendliest venue for performers. This was a place where Scarface and MC Lyte got booed off the stage. Its reputation had earned it the nickname "Apollo South."

That night a thug out of Liberty City's Pork-N-Beans projects took the stage and he stole the show. His name was Maurice Young, better known as Trick Daddy Dollars. Trick had just come home from a two-and-a-half-year bid in state prison. To see him tear down the Pac Jam and land himself a record deal was pretty inspiring. It got me thinking. *Maybe I could really do this.*

I ran into one of my old elementary school teachers not long after that. Miss Anderson. She was disappointed to hear I'd dropped out of college and when she asked what I was up to I told her I'd left school to become a rapper.

"You know, Will, my son has been making beats," she said. "I think you two should meet."

Miss Anderson's son was a kid named Rod. As a producer he went by the name Sharp Shoulders. For a high school freshman, he actually made some pretty good beats. He'd been learning his way around a mixing board at a new recording studio in Miami Lakes called Reel Sounds. It was owned by his cousin Earl. He invited me to come by and check it out.

From the minute I met Earl I knew he was getting a lot of money. Earl was dripping with diamonds. He had several chains, a diamond pinky ring, and a platinum Rolex iced-out with big-ass boulders all throughout the band and bezel. This was before everybody had bust-down Rollies. Parked outside the studio Earl had a '75 Chevy Caprice convertible sitting on chrome Daytons. Baby blue with white guts and a white rag top. It was one of several cars Earl owned.

Earl remembered me. He'd graduated from Carol City High in 1991 and had been friends with my sister's boyfriend at the time, a nigga named Griff. Griff had been a dope boy up until the day he got killed in Virginia so Earl's association with him was all the information I needed to know Earl was getting money in the streets.

Reel Sounds was Earl's legitimate business venture. He'd spent six figures building this state-of-the-art studio. It had hardwood floors, top-of-the-line recording equipment, and an upstairs lounge area and office. The place was real nice. After hearing me spit a few of my raps, Earl told me I was welcome to work out of his studio anytime.

Along with opening up the studio, Earl had started M.I.A. Productions, an independent record label. In his first attempts at discovering talent he'd come across a half Jamaican, half Puerto Rican teenager with matted up dreads freestyling in the pavilion of Carol City Park. His name was Richard Morales Jr., better known as Gunplay.

Gunplay could rap his ass off but he was a loose cannon. Gun was only sixteen but he had already dropped out of school, gotten locked up, and was slinging *and* snorting powder. He was trying to figure out his direction. Was he going to be a dope boy, a robber or a rapper? I liked Gunplay and took him under my wing. Soon we were together every day, at the studio and in the streets.

I'd been writing raps since elementary school but Earl's studio is where I cut my teeth as a songwriter. Prior to that point I would write these fifty-bar verses, string three of them together with no chorus and think that was a song. Now that I was working out of a real recording studio alongside other emcees, producers and engineers, I started tightening up all my verses to sixteen bars. I became mindful of how I wanted my voice to sound on wax and started layering my vocals and doing ad-libs. I recruited my old friend Bishop—my former collaborator on "Where the Hoes at?"— and got him to lay down choruses. Bishop had grown up singing in the church and he could harmonize real good.

Gunplay, Bishop and I came together to form a group called Triple C's, aka the Carol City Cartel. I was Willow, the pure lyricist of the group. Bishop had the ghetto gospel. And Gunplay was the wild card. He was Miami's version of Ol' Dirty Bastard. You never knew what you were going to get with him.

The original incarnation of Triple C's didn't last long. I soon realized we were going to have to find a replacement for Bishop. Bishop had a lot of talent but then could not stay out of trouble. He was going in and out of jail so much that it was impossible for us to get any momentum going as a group.

I was at the studio one day when a girl called saying she had a younger brother who could spit. His name was Torch. Earl had been putting up signs around the neighborhood advertising Reel Sounds and looking for talent. When she put Torch on the phone and he started rapping I was blown away. Big sis wasn't lying. Torch's punchlines were vicious and his flow was lethal. At first Gunplay didn't believe that Torch had really written his bars so we told him to come by the studio to see if he was for real.

From our phone call I knew that Torch was not from Miami. Niggas from the crib tend to talk and rap slow and Torch had the vernacular and delivery of a New York nigga. When he got to the studio he gave us his whole story. Torch was from the Castle Hill housing projects in the Bronx. He'd gotten caught up in some street shit and his mother had sent him to live with his sister in Fort Lauderdale. He'd been laying low there, but like the rest of us, he was trying to make something happen in the rap game.

From that day forward Triple C's was Gunplay, Torch and me. We started locking in at the studio every night. We had Sharp Shoulders and a couple other producers—shout-out to Ree Dog and Troy Bell—cooking up beats and Earl would be in there flexing all the money he was getting. Earl liked to stunt on us back then. Like Earl, I had a blue Chevy Caprice, except mine was a raggedy-ass four-door with wheels that looked like they could fall off at any minute. My granddaddy had given me that car. I remember one time there were some hoes chilling at the studio and Earl started clowning Gunplay for his clothes. Both of them had football jerseys on that day, except Gunplay's was a screen-printed replica jersey and Earl's was the authentic one with the stitched-on numbers and lettering. Earl had jokes about that too. He was throwing salt in the game! But look, I have nothing but love and respect for my big homie Earl. All of that stuff was petty shit. Earl opened the doors to his studios and gave me and Triple C's an opportunity when he didn't have to and there was nothing in it for him.

Eventually we had a collection of songs we felt pretty good about. We put together a mixtape and got a few hundred copies pressed up at Kinko's. At first we tried selling them but that didn't work. Miami didn't have an established market for mixtapes like Houston, where you could damn near go platinum selling tapes out of the trunk of your car.

We switched up the strategy and started giving the tapes away for free, handing them out at every flea market, strip club and after-hours spot from West Palm Beach on down. We'd slip DJs a couple dollars to get them to play our records, hoping that one of them would catch on in the clubs. But that didn't yield great results either. The problem wasn't just that people in Miami didn't buy mixtapes. The real issue was that Miami didn't really support its up-and-coming artists unless you were coming into the game with a cosign from Luke.

The plan was to keep grinding in hopes of getting the attention of an A&R or exec of a major label. If we could get a deal *then* the city would get behind us. It didn't matter if it was a group deal for Triple C's or if one of us got a solo deal. Earl never had any of us under contract. There was just an unspoken understanding that when one of us took off they would come back and bring everybody else with them. The problem was that none of us were going to be taking off anytime soon.

Things were moving pretty slow on the music front. The streets were a different story. Things were accelerating for me. Fast.

To reach that next level of hustling you had to go out of town. Cocaine was so cheap and in such abundance in Miami that it was hard to move a lot of weight there. Everybody had access to it and the competition was ferocious. This was especially true for Carol City niggas. Carol City wasn't like Liberty City and Overtown, where there were these huge projects you could stand outside of and sell dope all day. With the exception of the Matchbox and the apartments behind my house, Carol City was made up mostly of single-family houses. There was only so much money to be made here.

Big Mike had left Miami a long time ago. The crib had been ground zero for the Miami Boys but once law enforcement took notice they headed north, taking over every city in the Sunshine State, setting up traps all over the Southeast United States. Georgia, Alabama, Tennessee, Louisiana, Kentucky, the Carolinas, all the way up to Virginia. It was Colonialism 101.

Mike had tried to keep Jabbar and I out of the streets but once he realized that wasn't happening he took the opposite approach. If we were going to be doing this anyway, we would be better off doing it under his supervision and away from the violence that was happening in Miami. Mike had set Jabbar up with an apartment in Atlanta and a kilo and let his boy take it from there. Jabbar didn't need much guidance. If you give a Delancy some dope, they're going to know what to do with it.

Mike had evaded capture by not getting greedy. He would hustle in one place for six months and then take six months off. Then he would start up again someplace else. His strategy had not only kept him one step ahead of the law, but also built an expansive clientele all over the Southeast.

Mike started sending me to places on assignments, all of which involved the transportation of either drugs or money. There was the occasional gun run but that was only a few times. The instructions were simple. Get a car. Not the same one as before. Pick up. Deliver. It wasn't brain surgery but it did keep me busy. I started taking trips up and down I-95 on a regular basis, from Miami all the way up to the Carolinas.

One of the things that separated Mike and Jabbar from the other hustlers I came up around was that they were in the boy business. Most of my dealings with heroin took place in Jacksonville, where the demand for it was as big as it was in Miami but with very few people that had access to it. I started bringing it up to Jacksonville from Miami. I'd usually chill up there for a few days while niggas worked off the pack to get me the money to bring back home. But I really didn't like being around that shit. I never did heroin but I felt like I could have gotten addicted to it just from being in the same room and inhaling that shit while they chopped it up with chemicals like quinine and mannitol. If I was around the boy for a few days and then went home my stomach would start to hurt. That happened to me a few times. I was basically going through minor withdrawal.

Then there were the testers. Whenever I sold heroin the buyer would bring a tester to let them know what the vibe was. I'll never forget this one nigga. He claimed to have six sets of eyes and whenever he got on boy he would see all this wild shit and tell us about it. To be honest, the nigga was hilarious but the whole scene was so fucked up. I can't quite put my finger on why but everything about dealing with heroin was more disturbing to me than it was with crack. The dealers. The junkies. The feeling of selling it for days on end. The only thing I really liked about it was the money. That money from the boy comes faster.

What started as courier work soon led to me branching out and building my own customer base. I started networking in the different cities I was bringing work to. I'd go to the strip clubs and meet girls who would know a local dope boy in need of a Miami plug. Then the next time I'd go to these places I wasn't just there as a driver. I had my own clients there.

I found a foothold in the Florida Heartland where I had cousins on my daddy's side. I drove up there one time to bring one of them some work and realized Central Florida was ripe for the taking. Soon I started taking trips up the Florida Turnpike and going to places like Bartow and Belle Glade and Melbourne and Okeechobee. These were untapped markets where I could set the price. I could run these country spots!

> I took a quarter ki to Polk County
> All my Central Florida niggas straight 'bout it
> Broke down the brick, I'm back in Bartow
> Belle Glade, box Chevy, on my car phone
> J-Ville, I went and bought a condo
> Back to the crib where I get it by the carload
>
> —"Box Chevy" (2013)

Even after I struck out on my own and started making my own plays I knew that I was a part of something that was much bigger than me.

When it comes to music, I can say with confidence that I am

self-made. But as far as the dope game, I have to admit that I was a beneficiary of nepotism. From day one I had friends in high places. All of the groundwork was laid out for me. I was a part of something. A system that had been in place long before I got there. I just kept building on it.

CHAPTER

6

1998 WAS A MAJOR TURNING POINT. THE
feds started coming down on everybody. Hard.

Things had been headed that way for a while. Ronald Reagan's War on Drugs fucked up the streets. The Sentencing Reform Act of 1984 had eliminated parole and established mandatory minimums requiring offenders to serve at least 85 percent of their sentences. Two years later, at the height of the crack epidemic, Congress passed the Anti-Drug Abuse Act, mandating a minimum sentence of five years for possession of five grams of crack. But you had to have more than five hundred grams to get the same sentence if you were caught with the powder.

A small amendment to the Anti-Drug Abuse Act in 1988 put a lot of my homies behind bars. The conspiracy amendment made it so that every person involved in a conspiracy could be held accountable for every crime committed within that conspiracy. Now the lookout boy or the bomb man were getting the same sentences as the kingpin. Due to case-processing de-lays in the courts, the impact of these laws wasn't fully felt until the nineties. That's when niggas started doing a lot of snitching.

But it wasn't just the weight niggas was moving that even-tually did them in. It was also the bodies they were dropping.

On September 6, 1992, Boobie got shot five times in the parking lot outside of Club Rollexx, an infamous Miami strip joint. They said Boobie tried to give it to some nigga but his gun jammed and the guy gave it to him instead. Boobie had scars all across his stomach and had to wear a colostomy bag after that.

My corner so polluted, young niggas lootin'
I studied Kenneth Williams, I'm one hell of a student
Remarkable hustle, my nigga's coming home
I kept a candle lit, my nigga never rolled
Niggas caught him slippin', gave him a shitbag
Five shots to the stomach, Tupac gift pack

—"Mafia Music III,"
Mastermind (2014)

Like the Dadeland Mall shooting in '79, the shootout at Rol-lexx triggered an era of violence *The Miami Herald* dubbed "A Decade of Death." Once these rival gangs declared war on each other—the Boobie Boys in Carol City, the Thomas Family in River City, the John Does in Liberty City, the Vondas in Overtown—Dade County became a combat zone. They started going tit for tat with the killings. On any given day, at any given moment, cars full of niggas with sticks were riding around the city looking for an enemy to open fire on.

In 1996 and '97 Miami was the murder capital of the United States. The headlines prompted the formation of a federal task force to put an end to the bloodshed. Their investigation gave birth to the whole "Boobie Boys" thing. That was a name the government came up with so that they could go after all their targets together under the umbrella of organized crime, instead of having to figure out all these unsolved shootings on a case-by-case basis. Boobie had been a mentor of mine, and we made plays together, but I was never some lieutenant under him or part of any gang. It just didn't work like that.

On February 23, 1998, the task force released the findings of their investigation, pinning thirty-five homicides and more than a hundred shootings on the gang wars between the Boobie Boys, the Vondas, the Thomas Family and the John Does. When the federal indictment came down a month later, Boobie did the one thing I'd never seen him do. He ran.

Four months later the feds rushed Jabbar's trap in Southside Jacksonville. I missed that raid by the skin of my teeth. I'd been in Jacksonville the week before. The indictment implicated Big Mike, Jabbar, his cousin Tarvoris, and a few others in a decades-long conspiracy to distribute cocaine and heroin throughout the Southeast United States. The way the feds were telling it, Jabbar had followed in his daddy's footsteps and taken over the family business.

I found out what happened through 30. 30 was me and Jabbar's little homie. He'd gone to school with J at Miami Central and had been running with us in Jacksonville. He was riding shotgun in Jabbar's Chevy when it all went down. They had gotten tipped off by one of Mike's former accomplices that the feds were coming. He'd met up with them and lifted his shirt up to show he was wearing a wire. But we never trusted this guy. J thought he was trying to get them to flee the trap so that he could go take the stash or the money they had buried in the back. Jabbar's plan was to go to over there, pick up the money and then get out of town for a little while, to be safe. But when they got to the house there were agents everywhere. 30, being the wild nigga he is, was ready to take them on a high-speed but Jabbar told him to pull over. There was nowhere to run. They had them.

The feds brought 30 in for questioning but he wasn't listed in the indictment. They confiscated the five bands he had on him but eventually let him go. But before they did that they asked him about me. Throughout the course of their surveillance the feds had seen 30 and Jabbar coming and going with a big black fat nigga in a truck. That was my car. A two-tone candy-painted Dodge Ram 1500 on seventeen-inch chrome Daytons.

With everything that was going on it was too hot for me to be in Florida. I had to get the hell out of Dodge. 30 was in need of a place to lay low as much as I was and he said he had an older sister in Marietta, Georgia, where we could stay at. We picked up one of 30's buddies, Kase, and were on our way.

When we got to the house we were greeted by Tomcat, 30's brother-in-law. At the time he opened his doors to us, Tomcat didn't know that we were on the run and he most definitely didn't know that we would end up sleeping on his floor for the next three months.

30 convinced Tomcat to let us stay with him by pitching him on these two buddies of his who rapped. Tomcat was working as a runner for some ambulance chaser lawyer at the time but he was a self-taught audio engineer and he was trying to make a lane for himself in Atlanta's rap scene. He wanted to put Kase and I together in a group called The Connect.

I wasn't too interested in being in another group. I already had Triple C's. But Kase had a bit of a buzz back home. He'd gotten a feature on Trick Daddy's last album. That made him much more established than I was. Aligning myself with Kase might be not be a bad idea.

One of the lawyers Tomcat worked with claimed to have a line on Shaquille O'Neal. This was when Shaq was in the rap game and had his own imprint under Universal Records called T.W.Is.M. (The World Is Mine). I figured this lawyer was fronting but he actually came through and arranged for us to meet Shaq at the All-Star Cafe on Peachtree Street.

Kase and I took turns freestyling for Shaq for over an hour. With every punchline I dropped, Shaq was getting more and more excited. One line in particular most definitely got his attention.

I'll hit you knee high, slap you straight out your fucking Filas!

Shaq stood up from his chair and took a lap around the restaurant after that one.

We left that dinner meeting convinced that The Connect would soon be offered a deal at T.W.Is.M. But a week later the lawyer Tomcat had been in touch with got indicted on money laundering charges. Tomcat wasn't able to get back in touch with Shaq's manager and that was pretty much the end of that. The Connect fizzled out soon after and Kase went back to Miami.

The T.W.Is.M. situation had been a bust but Tomcat soon introduced me to two important players in my early music career, DJ Greg Street and Russell "Big Block" Spencer.

Greg Street is best known as the host of *The Greg Street Show* on Atlanta's urban radio station V-103. He's hugely influential in Southern hip-hop and has had a hand in a lot of success stories that have come from below the Mason-Dixon line.

The same can be said about Block. Niggas know Block as the founder of Block Entertainment, the label behind Boyz N Da Hood and Young Joc, but this is way before any of that. I was first introduced to Block because I was looking for a weed connect in Atlanta.

Block had good weed but he also had a lot of connections. Block used to hang with Tupac and the Outlawz back when Pac was living in Atlanta, and he took me to meet Pac's cousin Kastro. Then he brought me to Noontime Studios where I met and started building relationships with industry players like Henry "Noonie" Lee, Ryan Glover and Chris Hicks. Block plugged me in with a lot of people in Atlanta.

The most important person Block and Greg Street introduced me to at this time was Tony Draper. Tony Draper was the founder of Suave House, the Houston-based label behind the rise of artists like 8-Ball and MJG, Crime Boss, Tela and South Circle. Draper had partnered with Block and Greg Street to help him establish a Suave House presence in Atlanta. He could see the city was bubbling with talent and fitting to blow. Draper was in the process of building a Suave House satellite office in Dunwoody but in the meantime he'd set up a recording studio in Greg Street's basement at his house in Stone Mountain.

Greg Street had Tristan "T-Mix" Jones staying with him. T-Mix was the in-house producer for Suave House and the genius behind the signature Memphis sound on all the early 8-Ball and MJG albums I'd come up listening to. That smooth, fly, player pimp shit.

Greg told me that I was welcome to work out of his studio and as soon as he extended that invitation I knew I'd be there every day until somebody told me to stop coming. I was such a big fan of 8-Ball and MJG, and the opportunity to record alongside T-Mix was something I had to take full advantage of. It would be the first time I worked with someone who knew more about making music than I did.

Greg Street's hospitality extended beyond free studio time. I would raid his fridge for food, and on nights that Tomcat needed a break from hosting me, Greg would let me spend the night.

Block was managing an artist named Lil Noah and had gotten Tony Draper to sign him to Suave House. Noah had talent but he was pretty green when it came to songwriting so

I started helping him put records together. Draper eventually caught wind that there was some big nigga in Greg Street's basement writing all of Noah's raps. So he flew out to Atlanta to see what this Teflon Don cat was all about. That was the name I was going by at the time. I'd repainted my Ram truck purple with ghost flames and gotten "Teflon Don... Album Coming Soon" painted on the side.

I was surprised to see that Draper was so young. He was only a year older than me but had already accomplished so much in the game. It's one thing to do that as an artist. Rapping is a young man's sport. But as an executive and CEO? To come up out of the mud and do it all independent? That shit was impressive.

I was working with Noah on a song called "Bird Bath" when Draper showed up to the studio. He heard me lay my verse on there and it was all he needed to hear. As soon as I stepped out of the booth he told me he wanted to sign me to Suave House.

"What's your name?"

"Teflon Don," I told him.

"You're my next 8-Ball, Tef," he said. "You're the next Biggie."

After I signed to Suave House, Draper started bringing me city to city, taking me to different music conferences and introducing me to his network in the industry. He had quite the Rolodex.

Draper took me out to Houston's Fifth Ward, where I got to meet and play basketball with J. Prince in the middle of the night. J. Prince was the founder of Rap-A-Lot Records and as far as I was concerned, he was as much of a pioneer as Luke. J. Prince was the inspiration for a sixteen-year-old Tony Draper to launch Suave House and he paved the way for niggas like Master P to launch No Limit Records and for Bryan "Birdman" Williams and his brother to launch Cash Money Records. Rap-A-Lot was the blueprint for building an independent hip-hop label in the South.

Draper knew that meeting a Southern king like J. Prince

was a dream come true for me but he wanted to get me rapping over some East Coast beats. So he flew me out to New York to work with Redman and Erick Sermon. Redman picked me up at the airport in his BMW X5 truck. I couldn't believe it was him that came to get me. Red was riding high from the success of *Doc's Da Name 2000* and *Blackout!*, two critically acclaimed, platinum-selling albums.

Before we headed out to Erick Sermon's crib in Long Island, we stopped in Harlem to pick up a jar from Branson. Branson was the infamous weed man to the stars. I'd heard his name in the raps of Redman, Biggie, Ma$e and Rakim. He was the inspiration behind "Samson," the drug dealer character in a new stoner comedy called *Half Baked*, starring Dave Chappelle.

I hadn't been in New York an hour and everything about it was surreal. I was really here sitting in the back of Redman's truck. We'd just picked up weed from Branson and now we were on our way over to Erick Sermon's house. Redman was a bona fide superstar at this time but the fact that I was about to cut a few records in The Green Eyed Bandit's basement was what really fucked me up. I came of age in rap's golden era and EPMD had a major influence on me. I'm getting ahead of myself here but my whole "Maybach Music" series of songs was inspired by EPMD's "Jane" saga, where every album they put out had a new song that continued the "Jane" character's storyline.

As we rode past Shea Stadium I remember taking a second to let the moment sink in.

This ain't no regular shit, homie. This means something. Make it count.

One of the records we did that week, "Ain't SHHH to Discuss," would end up on Erick Sermon's 2000 album *Erick Onasis*. It would be my first placement on a major-label album. E-Double's still got an unreleased record we did back then I know would still fuck people up if they heard it today. I'd be remiss if I didn't mention that. We'll get that Michael Jackson sample cleared one day, big homie.

It was after one of these trips that Draper told me he had a surprise for me. When I got home there was a package. I opened it up and almost shed a tear. He'd sent me a Rolex watch. It was my first, and it wasn't a bust-down. It wasn't a plain Jane either. It was iced-out, with real Rolex diamonds. That bitch was mint.

I have always loved watches. I consider myself to be a collector of timepieces. When I was young I could only afford Geneva and Guess. Those were the days I used to daydream about the Breitling Emergency watch that would send a helicopter to your location if you pulled the pin out. Once I got money I started collecting them. I got the Audemars Piguet that Arnold Schwarzenegger wore in *Terminator 3*. Dr. Dre once gave me a $100,000 Hublot as a birthday present and Drake once gifted me a Presidential Rolex.

But none of those watches hold the same sentimental value as the Rolex Tony Draper gave me in 2000. The watch wasn't an advance. It wasn't his way of paying me back for something. There were no strings attached to it. It was just a gift that came from the goodness of his heart. A way of showing his appreciation for me as his artist and as his friend.

Draper didn't know how much the gift meant to me. That's because I never let him know how broke I was. After Jabbar got indicted I'd decided to fall back from the streets a little bit and try to dedicate myself to my music. That decision had hurt my pockets. The little money I did have I put toward keeping up appearances. I kept myself looking fresh and I always had a nice ride. At some point I turned in my show truck and got the new Cadillac Escalade. But my life was nowhere near as glamorous as I made it out to be.

When I would go out to Houston to see Draper I would have to sleep in my car because I didn't have money for a hotel.

Draper would take me around and introduce me to all these legends of the game and I looked like I belonged among them. When Scarface pulled up on us in his black 600 Benz outside the Sharpstown Mall on the southwest side of Houston—right at the corner of Fondren and Bellaire Boulevard—I didn't feel out of place. I looked like an established artist. But at night I would find a rest area on the highway to pull over and knock out for a few hours. When I woke up I'd meet back up with Draper acting like I'd just left the fucking St. Regis.

Draper would have never allowed that to happen if he knew that I needed a place to stay. But I didn't want him to know that. I didn't want to look like a beggar with my hand out. Even when I first met Draper and I was sleeping in Greg Street's basement, I'd given off the impression that I was this big boss rich nigga. I had him fooled too.

CHAPTER

7

A FEW MONTHS HAD PASSED SINCE THE feds grabbed Jabbar, and I figured it was safe for me to start making a couple plays again back home. I needed the money. The problem was all my main partners were out of the picture. Jabbar was locked up and Big Mike and Boobie were on the run. That series of events fucked up the whole ecosystem of Miami's dope game.

Mike had changed his appearance and fled the country. He'd switched out the curly perm for a high top fade and taken his golds out. He was hiding out in the Bahamas with his cousin Samuel "Ninety" Knowles. Samuel was an even bigger kingpin than Mike and he had cribs all over the Caribbean. When the indictment came down, Mike left the US and started island-hopping from one place to the next.

Boobie remained stateside, and we stayed in contact even after he skipped town. Sometimes I'd drive up to Atlanta where he was laying or he'd slip into Miami for a minute and come see me. I could hardly recognize Boobie then. He'd switched up his whole appearance. I was used to seeing Boobie dressed fresh from his New Era fitted down to his white Air Force Ones but now he was dressed like a nerd. Boobie used to have the Ford Mustang 5.0 GT convertible that Kane drove in *Menace II Society* but now every time I saw him he was in a different car. Never anything that would attract attention. Always something inconspicuous.

With my day ones out of pocket, I started running with a new crew. Earl was getting money with a crew out of the Venetian Gardens housing projects. This group of guys—Kane, Black Bo, Short Legs, Skinny—were cool with a lot of the niggas I knew from the Matchbox, being that they all repped 37th Avenue. They came up under Big Mike too. Soon we became close friends and partners in crime.

This is also around the same time I started dealing with Wayne Parker. Wayne was an associate of Boobie's and he had a big-ass crib in northwest Dade County, where my sister and her friends used to hang out at. I'd known of Wayne for a while but we didn't start doing business together until my homie Troy brought me and Jabbar over to his house one day.

In God's name, free Troy Payne
Since he was jailed, Carol City ain't been the same
Seventeen years old, floating on gold thangs
Insane Payne was my nigga's code name

—"Hold Me Down,"
Rise to Power (2007)

Troy was Wayne's protégé. At the time—we're talking '97 or maybe early '98—me, Jabbar and Troy all had four-wheeler ATVs. We would raise hell on our banshees. We'd ride through the city doing donuts, popping wheelies and swerving in and out of traffic. When the police would show up we'd take them on a high-speed. Just getting the city police to come after us wasn't shit though. We'd take it to that next level and get on the highway to try to get the Florida Highway Patrol's attention. That meant the radio call was going out across the state!

On this particular chase, we had been zooming down the turnpike and peeled off at the exit near Joe Robbie Stadium. We cut through a couple side streets and once we knew we'd lost them Troy brought us over to Wayne's house. Wayne had a big ass crib with these intricate Roman porch columns in the front. His lawn was immaculate and sitting behind the gates was a full-on fleet. There were multiple Benzs. The two-door S500 and the big body four-door one too. I knew those ran $150,000 a pop. Then he had the black cherry Chevy Tahoe sitting on dubs. A blue-on-blue '75 Chevy drop-top. Fully-loaded BMWs and Acuras. There must have been ten whips out there. To this day the way that I line up my cars outside my homes is based on how I saw WP living in the nineties.

Wayne walked out the house in a silk robe. He had a glass of champagne in one hand and a joint of some crip in the other. Wayne always had the best weed. Before I met him I had only ever smoked Reggie and Jamaican yard weed. Wayne was the first to put me onto the highpower shit. On his wrist he had a $100,000 platinum Rolex. The only two niggas I'd ever seen with that watch were Puff Daddy and Sisqo. WP was a flamboyant playboy.

"How y'all youngsters doing?"

"We just shook the crackers!"

"Well y'all enjoy yourselves and be safe. You let me know if you need anything from me."

I didn't start doing business with Wayne until Troy went to prison in '98. Boobie and Mike were both on the run so I kind of slid into Troy's position as Wayne's understudy and Wayne took on the mentor role that I'd had in guys like Mike and Boobie.

But Wayne was a different character than Mike or Boobie.

Wayne was not a gangster. He was never involved in any of the violence those two were always embroiled in. None of the shit that leads to bodies getting dropped—robberies and hitting licks and juugs—was in Wayne's DNA. His success came from being a smooth salesman and master chemist. There were very few niggas who knew how to cook crack as good as Wayne did. All his shit looked picture perfect and he never stepped on anything. He just sold a lot of dope peacefully and enjoyed the fruits of his labor.

Even though Wayne was no gangster he was so highly respected that nobody would ever try him. I remember one night a group of us were at Club Amnesia and got into it with some niggas. We were on the verge of pulling out pistols when Wayne stepped in the middle and told everybody to cool out. He didn't raise his voice or anything. He was real calm. And everybody acknowledged him. There were few niggas who could do something like that and the ones who did have that power were usually violent niggas. WP was ahead of his time.

I thought the feds would never catch Big Mike. He was the last of the Miami Boys still on the run. His two partners, Causey "Silk" Bryant and Ike Florence, had been behind bars for years. Silk got sentenced to life in prison in 1989 and Ike received a twenty-eight-year sentence in 1993.

I didn't think the feds would catch Boobie either. He moved with the utmost caution. In all my years knowing Boobie I can't say he ever put a package in my hand. Not one time. I'd always stumble upon things someplace else. In the trunk of my car or in a trash can outside my house.

Mike and Boobie were so similar. Two Virgos who paid close attention to the smallest of details and made their moves methodically.

But in the spring of 1999 everybody's luck ran out. Mike had a momentary lapse in judgment that was the slipup the feds had been waiting on. He came back to Miami after becoming suspicious that his woman was cheating on him. Not only did he come back to the States but he went back to his house. That mistake was so unlike him. They got Mike on some weak shit.

They snatched Boobie in Clarkston, Georgia, a month later. Boobie didn't slip up like Mike had. The amount of attention on him just got to be too much. There was a $56,000 reward for information leading to his arrest and the *Miami Herald* was reporting on his manhunt every other week. After he was featured on episodes of *Crimestoppers* and *America's Most Wanted* it was only a matter of time. He was in a vise grip and couldn't move. There was too much heat on him.

Two weeks after the feds got Boobie I was with Wayne Parker at Studio Center in Miami Lakes. I was splitting my time between Atlanta and Miami and I was looking for a new place to record when I was at the crib. I wasn't recording at Earl's studio anymore.

But this was before there were home studios, so it was going to cost $155 an hour, plus an additional $55 for an engineer. That was for Studio Center's bare minimum C-Room. That's why I was trying to get Wayne to foot the bill for my studio time. Wayne knew I had talent and he was down to invest in my career. But he had some constructive criticism for me. He thought that I was rapping too fast and that I should dumb my bars down so people could understand my message.

It was raining when Wayne and I left the studio. It was June 1, 1999, the Tuesday after Memorial Day weekend. Hurricane season was starting up again. We smoked a joint and then Wayne dropped me off at my momma's house. The plan was to meet back up later that night with a few of our homies at a comedy show at in Coconut Grove. But when I got to our seats at The Improv, Wayne wasn't there.

"Fatboy, you heard about Wayne?"

My heart skipped a beat. In Miami when somebody starts

a sentence off with "You heard about…" that usually means someone is dead.

"What happened?"

"You was just with him, right?"

"Yeah."

"When he got back to his crib the Marshals were waiting for him. They said he caught an indictment out of Pensacola? I ain't ever know Wayne to go up there but you know how it go. Niggas been telling and the feds ain't playing fair."

After the feds extradited Mike to the pretrial detention center in Jacksonville, I drove up to see him and Jabbar. They had them housed in separate units so I visited Jabbar first. As soon as I sat down he put a stack of paperwork against the glass that separated us. It was his indictment.

Jabbar's indictment listed more than fifty unindicted co-conspirators. His momma was listed. His younger brother. His ex-wife. Well-known Miami dope boys like Rick "The Mayor" Brownlee were listed. Then I saw my name. It just said "Will, aka Fatboy."

Jabbar turned to the next page that showed the feds had had their eyes on us for a while. As I read through the report I realized we had noticed these guys watching us one night at The Silver Fox, a strip club on Jacksonville's west side. At the time we thought they were some jack boys plotting to rob us. We had walked up on them and pulled our pistols out. It never occurred to us they could be undercover agents.

"Look, they don't know who you are and I didn't fill in the blank for them," Jabbar told me. "But they know the truck."

"I ain't driving the truck no more. So what's the play?"

"Ain't no play."

There were so many inaccuracies in this indictment, which was completely based on statements from confidential informants.

Jabbar was born in 1976, the same year as me. But according to his paperwork he'd been running this massive multistate heroin ring since 1983. He would have been seven years old at the time.

"Your lawyer must be all over these mistakes, right?" I asked him.

"You really don't understand how this shit works until they come, Fatboy" Jabbar said. "And then it's too late."

When I went to see Mike he told me I needed to sit down for a while. He had no interest in seeing me taking up the torch.

"Go get a job somewhere. I ain't asking you, I'm telling you," he said. "Remember when I used to say only one out of a thousand hustlers make it? Go be a fireman or something."

I was pretty shaken up leaving the prison that day. Football hadn't worked out. College hadn't worked out. Now everybody was getting indicted. Jabbar had already accepted a plea deal. He was going to a dime in federal prison.

Six months later Mike was convicted of the same charges. They gave him thirty years. A few weeks after that they gave Wayne thirty-five. The way things were looking for Boobie, he was never getting out. Boobie's case was a whole different situation. He was dealing with bodies.

It felt like my whole world was caving in on me. Between Troy and Jabbar and now Mike and Boobie, my two closest friends and mentors had just vanished from my life. And then my father died.

In September the doctors told him they'd found a spot on his lung. Within months the cancer had spread to his liver. He had tumors the size of golf balls all throughout his body.

Being the computer nerd that he was I know my daddy would have wanted to make it to the new millennium and see how all the Y2K shit played out. But he didn't. He died in December. He was sixty-four years old.

Even though my father and I had been distant for years, I always knew that the love between us was there. He had moved to Mississippi to be near Renee and I knew one day I'd drive out there and we would chop it up and get back solid. It fucked me up that I was wrong about that.

Why did my father die so young? Was it all those years living near the phosphate mines? Was it the cigarettes? Or was it something else? I would never know. The unspoken words between us would remain unspoken. Because I didn't have the heart to be the one to initiate our reconciliation. To this day I wish I had.

I can hear my Daddy saying, "Lil nigga go get 'em!"
Passed in '99, cancer all up in his liver
Shit different since we last spoke, his son's a lil richer
I'll never rap again if I could tell him that I miss him
Why the fuck I own the world if I can't share it with him
Bust his ass his whole life, just want to break bread with him
Crying in my mansion as I'm holding on his picture
It's a cold and lonely world, I'm flying solo on you niggas

—"All the Money in the World,"
Teflon Don (2010)

Block drove out to Clarksdale with me for the funeral. I was in a lot of pain but there was a numbness to it. What I remember more than the sadness is how lost I felt. I was looking for guidance. But there was no one left to turn to. Everyone was gone. As I lowered my father's casket into his grave the same thought kept replaying in my mind.

What the fuck am I supposed to do?

CHAPTER

8

IT WAS BECOMING CLEAR MY SITUATION
at Suave House wasn't going anywhere. Draper was coming to
Atlanta less and less and then he stopped answering his phone.
I was recording a lot of music but there were no plans in place
for me to put out an album. I wasn't the only one. Draper had
signed a bunch of artists to Suave House around the same time
that he signed me—Noah, Gillie da Kid, Coo Coo Cal, Psy-
chodrama, the Ill Hillbillies—and none of us had release dates
on the horizon.

The writing was on the wall when I realized that Block and
Greg Street had moved on to other things. Block had given up
on Noah and taken a position as head of A&R at Noontime
Records. And Greg Street was working on a Southern rap compilation album for Atlantic Records called *Six O'Clock, Vol. 1.*
I was actually supposed to be on that project. Greg Street paid
me $5,000 for a song I did called "Willy Bananas" in what was

the first time I ever got paid for a feature. Greg didn't end up keeping me on the album—Atlantic wanted bigger names on the project—but he let me keep the five stacks.

The second chapter of Suave House had not gone well for Tony Draper. In 1998 Draper had played a part in helping close Cash Money Records' $30 million distribution deal with Universal Records. Draper wanted to start signing artists and dropping albums left and right the way Cash Money and No Limit Records were doing. But Universal wasn't interested in doing that with Suave House. They were only getting behind 8-Ball and MJG releases.

So in 1999 Draper exited his distribution deal with Universal and entered into a joint venture with Artemis Records, where he put out the 2000 Suave House compilation album *Off Da Chain, Vol. 1.* When that album flopped Draper got out of that deal and partnered with another label called JCOR Entertainment. That deal went even worse for him.

While Draper was tied up in a lawsuit with JCOR, his artists started defecting from Suave House. On top of all that Draper may have gotten caught up in some street shit too. I knew he wasn't trying to keep me on the shelf but I also knew I wasn't at the top of the priority list.

Nine times out of ten when a label's CEO gets jammed up the artists are going down with him. But Draper didn't want to see that happen to me. He wanted me to win whether it be at Suave House or someplace else. So before things got to a point where I could become disgruntled and start exploring my options, Draper approached me with an opportunity to sign with Slip-N-Slide Records.

Slip-N-Slide was not just the hottest label in South Florida. It was one of the hottest labels in the rap game, period. Founded in 1994 by Ted "Touche" Lucas, Slip-N-Slide became a local household name following the release of *Based on a True Story*, the 1997 debut album of Trick Daddy Dollars.

I'd first seen Trick Daddy at the Pac Jam back in '95, when he won that talent show and got himself a deal with Luke. But that deal never ended up coming together. Luke was forced to file for bankruptcy and let go of his whole roster. But what was a missed opportunity for Luke ended up being a blessing in disguise for Trick. Things were working out for him at Slip-N-Slide big-time. His second album, *www.thug.com*, had sold more than 500,000 copies, and its breakout single "Nann Nigga" introduced the world to a second Slip-N-Slide star. A bad bitch out of Liberty City named Trina.

Trick's success, coupled with the rise of Trina, elevated Slip-N-Slide's profile to a national level, leading to a major-label joint venture with Atlantic Records. But even though Slip-N-Slide was the shit, I had a lot of reservations about making the move over there.

For starters, I wasn't too interested in signing to a Miami-based label. I felt like I never got a lot of love at the crib when it came to my music. I'd put in a lot of blood, sweat and tears trying to get my career off the ground in Miami and I hadn't had much of a return on my investment.

Hip-hop in Miami was rooted in the up-tempo booty-shaking music of the Luke era. With the rise of JT Money and Poison Clan, followed by Trick and Trina's, the city's sound had begun to evolve. But it still wasn't what I was doing. Trick was the living, breathing incarnation of the Pork-N-Beans projects he came out of in Liberty City. He was rapping for the thugs with dookie dreads and permanent gold teeth. The niggas who laced their blunts with coke. We call it boonk.

I was a fat handsome nigga who wanted to be rich. I wanted to have a half a million dollar car and a three million dollar house and I wanted to have a pretty hoe in a bikini with me in the jacuzzi. You have to understand. Niggas in Miami were not rapping about any type of boss shit like that back then.

I was putting on for the city but my vision was bigger than Miami. Trick was the voice of niggas who were never leaving the projects. I couldn't limit myself to that. I couldn't just rap about donks. I had my eyes on the new Maybachs that Mercedes-Benz had just introduced. I couldn't just rap about wearing Dickies. I had visions of me at the Met Gala in silk Versace fabrics. I couldn't just rap about eating conch, mangos and Jamaican beef patties. I wanted marbleized tomahawk steaks from Del Frisco's.

There were all these things that were still outside my reach. Cars and clothes I couldn't buy yet. Places I'd never been. People I'd never met. These were the things that occupied my thoughts and kept me awake at night. Of course they became a part of my music. I was rapping my reality but I was also rapping my destiny. I was speaking things into existence.

The other cause for concern when it came to signing with Slip-N-Slide had to do with some old street shit. There was the potential for problems with Trick Daddy's camp. I didn't know T-Double personally and I was a fan of his music but there had been situations in the past involving Boobie and Trick's people that could make for lingering bad blood between us. When Trick's brother Hollywood got murdered in '94, word on the street was that Boobie had had something to do with it. Boobie always denied that was true but once the rumor began to spread a lot of people in the city accepted it as fact.

Hollywood hadn't just been Trick's brother. He was also best friends with Ted Lucas. The two of them had planned on launching a record label together. Plus Hollywood was dating Trina at the time of his death. So Slip-N-Slide was this tight-knit group built around the loss of a family member. I was wary of signing there if I might be viewed as an enemy because of my affiliation to Boobie.

But Draper was telling me that Ted wanted to sign me so maybe that wasn't the case. While he and Ted worked out a business arrangement, my big homie Kane took the initiative to see if we could make this partnership work on a personal level. Kane knew Josh, Ted's partner at Slip-N-Slide, and he arranged for us to meet one day at the Carol City flea market.

Josh was from North Glade, a section of Carol City located a little west of where I'd come up. We'd never crossed paths but we shared a lot of mutual friends and associates. My first impression of Josh was that he was a friendly and somewhat reserved individual. But Kane had tipped me off that Josh was very, very, very certified in the streets. Josh came from a long line of hustlers and he was a student of Versace Neal. Versace Neal may have been the richest nigga in the streets at the time. Neal was someone you only heard people talk about. You would never see him pulling up to any of the go-to spots for dope boys. He had too much money for that. So Josh was a Triple OG off that association alone. Over time I came to realize Josh's soft-spoken demeanor was a red herring. Josh was like Mike Tyson in the sense that if you only judge him by his gentle manner of speech, you have no idea of what he's capable of.

Josh and I chopped it up and a few days later he brought me to meet Trick at his studio. Trick played me a few songs off his upcoming album and we even got to talking about working on some music together. Once I sensed that there wasn't any pressure coming from his side I started to come around to the idea of signing with Slip-N-Slide. After Ted reached an agreement with Draper to buy me out of my Suave House contract I did just that.

The day after I signed to Slip-N-Slide Josh took me to Studio Center in Hialeah, where I met Duece Poppi, a rapper from Atlanta who was supposed to be the label's next artist to blow. Duece would later change his name to Whole Slab, so just know whenever I talk about Duece I'm talking about Slab and vice versa.

Duece and I got off to a rocky start. I wanted to make it clear that I was going to be the label's next artist out the gate. But I dropped my bad attitude when I found out Duece knew Boobie.

After Boobie fled to Atlanta he started hanging out with Duece's big homie, a guy named Dixie Fare. Dixie was another Miami nigga who'd moved up to Atlanta and his name rang bells in the crib. So I eased up on Duece and we became fast friends. But I was still intent on making an impact at Slip-N-Slide from the jump. Duece and I did a song that day where I spit a verse that got everyone in the studio's attention.

> We could move a certain way 'cause we rich
> Suede seats, no roof, custom six
> Fly out to New York just to fuck with chicks
> They like to hear a little game before they suck your dick
> Maybe ask a dumb question, you touched a brick?
> Have you ever fucked Trina? What the fuck is this?!
> Bring some dime bags, just enough to twist
> Sitting next to Spike Lee, Mookie fuck the Knicks
> Fall off in the tunnel, puffin' crip
> Niggas smile when they see me, they love the wrist
> I don't dance too much, you could hug the hip
> That Grey Goose mine but you could bust the Cris
> Talking too much, just above a snitch
> Sit back, be quiet, just thug a bit
> I make sure every bottle stay upside down
> Everybody in the circle fucked up by now!

—"Hey,"
Godzilla Pimpin' (2003)

Talking about fucking Trina on day one at Slip-N-Slide definitely raised a few eyebrows. I ended up softening the line to "Have you ever *seen* Trina?" but I'd gotten my point across. I was the label's new whiz kid. I was here to shake the whole operation up.

Josh managed Trina and they were starting up work on her second album, *Diamond Princess*. He'd heard about my pen game and thought that I could be an asset in the studio. After my work with Noah never amounted to anything I wasn't too excited in more ghostwriting, but if this was my way of paying dues and making myself valuable then so be it.

Soon I was with Josh every day, riding around to different studios throughout the city. Audio Vision and Circle House in North Miami. Rare Breed Studios in Carol City. Poe Boy Studios in Little Haiti. House of Fire on South Beach. What started with me writing for Trina soon turned into me working with every artist on Slip-N-Slide's roster.

My first big look was "Told Y'all." "Told Y'all" was a record I wrote for Trina at Cool & Dre's studio. Today you might find Cool and Dre in London producing for Jay-Z and Beyoncé but back then they were an unknown duo working out of a makeshift studio in Cool's momma's house.

Initially I recorded "Told Y'all" as a reference track. Something that Trina could use if she decided to move forward with the record. But when Ted heard the song he thought I sounded so good on there he told me to write another verse for myself.

It was already a big deal to land a placement on Trina's album and it got even bigger from there. "Told Y'all" got chosen to be the lead single for the soundtrack to *All About the Benjamins*, a major motion picture starring Ice Cube and Mike Epps. I'd gotten myself a little cameo in one of Noah's videos but "Told Y'all" was my proper big-budget music video debut.

I was at Studio Center one day when I met a twenty-five-year-old producer from Chicago by the name of Kanye West. Kanye was working with another artist down the hall. We both had our own sessions going on but during our breaks we got to talking and he played me some of his beats. This was the chipmunk soul era of Kanye's sound and I loved the way he was chopping up samples.

Kanye ended up working out of Studio Center that whole week and we kept up our routine of having these little cyphers during our breaks. He'd play his beats and I'd spit my raps over them. By the end of the week Kanye was telling me he wanted to executive produce my whole album. I wasn't ready to commit to all that just yet but I definitely wanted to get me some of his beats. Kanye's beats were cheap then.

I ended up getting two of them. One was for me—a real soulful joint that sampled a song called "I'm Just Doin' My Job"—and one for Trina. That one became her hit single with Ludacris called "B R Right."

I caught up with Kanye a couple of months later at the Diplomat Resort in Hollywood on the set of the "B R Right" music video. We were both hanging around the set hoping to get cameos, which we did. You can see Kanye stepping off Ludacris's tour bus in the beginning and then toward the end I hop out of a taxi cab. If you even blink you'd miss either of us.

It was hardly the moment in the spotlight we both felt ready for. Kanye had gotten a lot of praise for his work on Jay-Z's album *The Blueprint* but his aspirations went beyond being the in-house producer at Roc-A-Fella Records. Kanye wanted to rap but the label wasn't taking him seriously. Meanwhile I was making plays at Slip-N-Slide but they weren't my own plays. I was still tossing other people alley-oops. "Told Y'all" had been a good look for me but there hadn't been any follow-through to capitalize on it.

Before we parted ways Kanye and I made plans to get back in the studio together soon. But the week before we were supposed to link up, I found out Kanye had been in a terrible car accident. He'd fallen asleep at the wheel after a late-night studio session in California and gotten into a head-on collision. He'd had reconstructive surgery on his shattered jaw, which was now wired shut, and he would be on bedrest for the foreseeable future. It would be eight years before me and Kanye crossed paths again.

In August of 2002 Slip-N-Slide had two major releases, Trina's *Diamond Princess* and Trick Daddy's *Thug Holiday*. Both debuted in the Top 20 of the Billboard 200 and would go on to be certified Gold by the Recording Industry Association of America.

Slip-N-Slide's reign was still going strong and I was proud to have played a part in its success. I'd written the two biggest singles off Trina's album and gotten three placements on Trick's. I'd proven myself to be a worthy acquisition. Now it was time to usher in the next big thing to come out of Miami. Rick Ross. I was ready to step out of the shadows. It was the only logical next step.

That's not how things played out. As part of Slip-N-Slide's joint venture with Atlantic Records, Atlantic had the first rights of refusal when it came to signing its artists. Atlantic had put up a small recording budget for me to record an album and I'd spent the last year working on it alongside the other projects I was working on for Slip-N-Slide.

But when Ted brought my album to Craig Kallman and Mike Caren, Atlantic's president and vice president of A&R, they weren't feeling it. They sent us back to the drawing board, saying I needed a more mainstream single.

For a minute there was one we felt pretty good about. It was produced by Saint Denson and sampled a 1977 Freda Payne song called "I Get High (On Your Memory)." Unfortunately I wasn't the only one to hear the beat. Somehow it got to Styles P of The LOX and his people at Interscope were able to secure the record with Styles being the much more established artist at the time. That song ended up being huge for Styles.

After that song fell through we went with another attempt at a single called "Just Chillin," which featured Trick, Kase and Gunplay. It didn't move the needle. At that point Mike Caren told Ted that Atlantic wasn't interested in putting any more money behind me. They were all set on Rick Ross. Without their backing I was told I basically had to throw my album in the trash. Just like that the rug had been yanked out from underneath me. I was pretty much back to square one.

I later learned that Craig and Mike had come back to Miami and signed Pretty Ricky. I'd been passed over for an R&B boy band. That news gutted me.

Underneath my jealousy I was genuinely happy for Pretty Ricky. Those boys had been doing their thing since the late nineties and they'd paid their dues too. We would perform the same circuit sometimes. The HBCU homecomings and TJ's DJ's music conferences. I always got a kick out of their choreographed performances and seeing the hoes lose their minds. The stage would be covered in glitter after their shows. On top of that, Blue, the boys' father and manager, was somebody well respected in the crib. I was never going to be anything other than supportive of their success. They deserved it.

But in my mind a panic had started to set in. Was I ever going to catch a break?

Those crackers chose Pretty Ricky over me... Oh my God... Oh my fucking God.

CHAPTER
9

I WAS STILL SIGNED TO SLIP-N-SLIDE BUT we were not on good terms. I felt like as soon as the situation with Atlantic went south, Ted went back to focusing on his two breadwinners, Trick and Trina. That didn't go over well with me.

This was when E-Class became my manager. E-Class was the founder of Poe Boy Entertainment, a local independent label. I'd known E-Class since I was in middle school but he was no-where near music then. When I first met E-Class he was doing two things: selling crack and cutting hair. He was friends with Renee and whenever he took a break from trapping out of the apartments behind my house he would come over and hang out. I had E buzz a Louis Vuitton logo into my hairline before my junior prom.

E got heavy in the streets prior to starting Poe Boy. In '93 he got indicted on conspiracy charges up in Tallahassee. But unlike most of the niggas I knew who caught cases around that time, E-Class beat his. He took his acquittal as a sign to pursue a more legitimate career.

The name "Poe Boy" was a tribute to a fallen soldier, a close friend of E-Class's named Kenin "Poe" Bailey. I knew Poe too. He lived a real turbulent street life. He and E-Class had had plans to get into the music game together but they needed start-up money. So Poe came up with a scheme to stick up a check-cashing store in Miramar right around the time that people were getting their tax refund checks. Poe had an inside man in the building, a barber who worked next door. Poe climbed into the ventilation system through a ceiling panel in the barbershop and waited above the check-cashing spot all night. When the employee showed up to work the next morning Poe dropped down like Tom Cruise in *Mission: Impossible* and told him to put all the money in the bag.

But the dude fought back and the whole lick went left. The police showed up on the scene and Poe made a run for it. He tried to steal one of the cruisers. He got shot several times before he was able to peel off. The chase didn't last long. Poe was bleeding out. He crashed the car and it was over with. They airlifted him out of there but he died before the helicopter landed at Jackson Memorial Hospital.

E-Class recruited two of his younger brothers—Chuck and Freezy—to help him get Poe Boy off the ground. Chuck was the numbers guy. He'd worked as a mortgage broker at Barnett Bank in Miami Lakes. Freezy would discover and manage another big artist to come out of Carol City, Flo Rida, after he married one of Flo's seven sisters.

E-Class didn't have the money to buy me out of my Slip-N-Slide contract and sign me to Poe Boy. All his resources were tied up in a female artist he was pushing named Jackie-O. So he became my manager instead. He and Alex "Gucci Pucci" Bethune, Poe Boy's vice president, took on the role of managing me on a day-to-day basis.

Josh was still the big homie but at that moment in time E-Class was a better fit to be my manager. E-Class was a Haitian silverback gorilla. He was willing to take an aggressive approach to advancing my career. We were well aligned that way. The way that I was feeling then. The way I was moving throughout the city. Aggression was my calling card. All of the disappointments had taken a toll on me and my patience had grown thin. I had a short fuse and niggas were getting slapped left and right over anything I perceived as disrespect. So I didn't need someone to politely ask DJs to play my music. I needed someone to tell them to. Someone who would go into a club or radio station and not leave until my record got played. E-Class was that guy.

For a nigga like E-Class, the rap game was more of a way for him to get money without having to go to prison. Pucci was more of a music aficionado. He was a little less rough around the edges and knew how to network in the industry beyond Miami. E-Class and Pucci each had their strong suits and as a pair they worked well together.

I stopped repping Slip-N-Slide and started dissing Ted and the label publicly, calling them "Slip-N-Slime" Records. Then I broke into Josh's studio and stole all the equipment and brought it to my garage. A crew of niggas showed up at my house to come get it back but Josh decided to let it slide. Not because he was afraid of me. He had more shooters behind him than I did. Josh just believed in me so much he still wanted to see me win. He'd rather take a loss than see me get knocked off over this. Josh knew I was acting out because I was frustrated.

I make music, I don't work for niggas
Ted Lucas jerkin' niggas
You on the phone, talking about what a hoe heard
It's not a good time, I ain't got no work

—"I Want to Talk to You,"
The Future of the South (2003)

In an interview with Larry Dog, a well-known Miami co-median, I was asked to give a piece of advice to up and com-ing artists. I looked straight into the camera and said, "Never sign a Ted Lucas contract." That video is still up on YouTube. Duece was standing there with me and you can tell he felt the same way I did. Ted hadn't put any money behind the release of *Godzilla Pimpin*. No music videos. No promotion. Nothing. Duece just wasn't as brazen as I was when it came to expressing those frustrations. I let my nuts hang.

Trick and I never ended up having problems over the street shit but tension did develop between us. I think Trick viewed me as a threat to his position as the top dog at Slip-N-Slide. To be fair, Trick wasn't doing the most egregious shit. It just didn't take much for me to go from zero to a hundred. Trick didn't pay me right away for opening for him one night so I ran up on him backstage and started talking about how I was the real "Mayor of Miami." Trick didn't want no problems.

Slip-N-Slide weren't the only ones in my crosshairs. I started dissing T.I. for calling himself the "King of the South." I was saying that that throne belonged to me but really I was jealous that he'd ended up with the beat for "Doing My Job," the re-cord I'd originally made with Kanye for my album. Now it was a song off *Trap Muzik*, a T.I. album just released by my friends at Atlantic Records.

You like the retarded kid, homie, we let you score
Mike Caren used his credit card for your next award

—"Rubber Band Man,"
Freestyle (2003)

If a radio DJ *didn't* play my songs then they were getting put
on blast. Go ask Big Lip Bandit and Supa Cindy, hosts of *The
Big Lip Morning Show* on 99 Jamz. I put out a dis saying all sorts
of foul shit about them. I actually had a crush on Supa Cindy.
I thought she was fine as hell. She was just a casualty of war.

Even DJ Khaled and I didn't meet on the best of terms. People know Khaled as one of my longtime friends and allies in
the music industry, but back then I viewed him as another gate-
keeper holding me back.

The Arab Attack. The Don Dada. The Big Dog Pitbull. Beat
Novacane. Khaled wasn't just another radio DJ spinning records
in the 305. He was *the* DJ and his cosign carried weight beyond
South Florida. Khaled was breaking records nationally. The energy he put into premiering a song made it feel like something
groundbreaking was taking place.

Khaled had earned his reputation as a tastemaker and his success story was against the odds. Born in New Orleans to Pal-
estinian immigrants, Khaled moved to Orlando as a teenager
before landing in Miami in the early nineties. Khaled had dib-
bled and dabbled in the streets a little bit—I think he used to
sell bootleg cell phones and did a bid in county jail for driving
with a suspended license—but his real passion was always music.

Khaled had been DJing high school dances back in Orlando
but it wasn't until he got to Miami that he started to build his
presence on the airwaves. He got his start spinning Caribbean
records on Miami's pirate radio station Mixx 96. After getting
the attention of Uncle Luke at a party he landed a job as cohost

of *The Luke Show* on 99 Jamz. When he got his own weeknight show there his career really started to take off.

I didn't give a fuck about any of that. What I cared about was that Khaled wasn't playing my music on the radio and he wasn't playing me in the clubs either. I resented him for it. On Saturday nights Khaled was the king at Club Krave. I'd be in there rolling on a bean—I was popping ecstasy regularly then—and when I wasn't dancing or tongue-kissing a random shone I'd see other rappers send drinks to the DJ booth to get Khaled to play their shit. I couldn't bring myself to go that route. Instead I put out a dis saying I had a stack for whoever brought me his Terror Squad chain.

Dissing Khaled and everybody else was my way of trying to get something going. I knew that Khaled wasn't trying to hold me back. On the few occasions we chopped it up I could see he was genuine in his attempts at constructive criticism. I just wasn't trying to hear it.

Burning bridges with the brass and trying to bully niggas into submission didn't do me any favors though. If anything, the extortion game did me a disservice. I was the malcontent of Miami more than I was the mayor. The city was not getting behind me. I was just so frustrated I didn't know how to act any different. I was burning out and looking for anything I could do to spark a flame.

This rap shit needed to work out soon or I was going to have to figure out something else. I was now the father of a beautiful baby girl, my daughter Toie, and her mother, Lastonia, was on my ass for money or else she was going to go the child support route. Lastonia and I were never in a real relationship. She and I were always friends more than anything else. But at that time we were arguing a lot.

My career was at a standstill. The most success I was seeing was with the ghostwriting. My work with Trina had opened the doors for me to work with several female artists. I wrote a song called "Nookie" for E-Class's girl Jackie-O, which ended up being a minor hit and led to Poe Boy landing a major label distribution deal. Then my big homie Kane connected me with a girl he found named Ashley Ross who Gunplay and I started working closely with.

I even got the opportunity to work with the queen of New York radio, Angie Martinez, at Audio Vision. Angie had just had a baby with the dude Nokio from Dru Hill and she still had her job at Hot 97 so she needed some help with her third album. For a little brown paper bag money and a piece of publishing I was more than happy to do so. Angie was real cool.

But that little money wasn't paying the bills. I was behind on my mortgage. I'd gotten a $30,000 advance from Slip-N-Slide and given all of it to my momma. She took it to Coldwell Banker and used it as a down payment for me to purchase my first home: a two-story, three-bedroom house in a gated community in Pembroke Pines. The good news was that I was a homeowner at twenty-four. The bad news was that I was house poor. Soon my momma was covering my mortgage and monthly car payment.

I thought after I signed to Slip-N-Slide that the money was going to start coming in left and right. That's why I blew the whole bag on the house. But now I was broke with no definitive source of income on the horizon.

Living in the red will take a toll on you. I was driving back to Miami one night after a show in Fort Myers. It was me, Gunplay, my homie P-Nut and Ashley Ross. All four of us were drunk and exhausted. None of us wanted to get behind the wheel or had any business doing so. But this show had only paid us $250 so we didn't want to have to spend the money we'd just made on a motel. It was only a two-and-a-half-hour drive back to

Miami. Somebody had to step up and take one for the team. And it wasn't going to be me.

"Nut, you ain't perform tonight," I said, tossing him the keys. "You're driving."

I dozed off in the passenger seat. Twenty minutes later I woke up to the sound of my Escalade's tires hitting the rumble strips. We were drifting off the highway. I looked over at P-Nut and he was out cold.

"Nut!"

By the time he opened his eyes it was too late. There was another car parked in the shoulder of the road and our front passenger side smashed into its rear end right as P-Nut cut the steering wheel, causing my car to flip. We flipped two or three more times until we finally stopped, landing upside down in the median.

My head was pounding and my ears were ringing but I could hear a hissing sound coming from the truck. The bitch was about to blow.

Gunplay, P-Nut and Ashley managed to wiggle their way out and took off running. But my ass was stuck. My door was completely caved in from the crash. I called out for Gunplay, who ran back and helped pull me out through the front windshield.

When the police showed up and asked who had been driving it was crickets. Nobody said a word. When they ran all of our licenses they came back and put me in handcuffs. Broward County had a warrant out for my arrest. Lastonia or one of my neighbors had called the cops on me after one of our fights. There weren't a lot of young black niggas living in my gated community so it didn't take much arguing for one of them to call the police.

I was placed in the back of a cruiser and taken to the local precinct. I wouldn't be there long. Gunplay got his momma and his pregnant girlfriend to drive up from Miami and bail me out.

They took two cars so that Gunplay's mom could put her 1995 Toyota Celica up as collateral.

As I sat in the holding cell I just kept shaking my head. I couldn't believe P-Nut had wrecked my car and that I had gone to jail behind it. I couldn't believe Lastonia had put a battery charge on me. I'd just talked to her the other day and everything seemed cool. This must have been from a while ago.

But those were the surface-level things I was angry about. Deep down I was pissed about where I was at in life. Suave House hadn't worked out. Slip-N-Slide wasn't working out. I'd just nearly lost my life and for what? Because I was too broke to spend the $250 I'd made performing at some bullshit club in Fort Myers.

It's hard to find friends as loyal as Gunplay. He pulled me out the car. He got his people to come bail me out. But I could see he was ready to walk away from music. The only reason he'd kept at it so long was because of his loyalty to me. Whatever I was with, Gunplay was with. That's how he is. But something needed to change. The way things were going, it just wasn't worth it.

CHAPTER

10

TO SAY THAT I WAS NOT WHERE I WANTED to be would be an understatement. It had been ten years since I dropped out of college to pursue music. Ten years of penning raps for other artists. Ten years of sleeping in my car and on friends' floors. A decade of waiting my turn and watching other niggas blow. And here I was. Still waiting.

The crackers at Atlantic weren't the people to pass on me. After his own working relationship with Suave House ended, Block had started working with Puff Daddy. Block knew Puff's girlfriend Kim Porter and she had connected them. Like I said before, Block knows everybody.

Puff had launched a Bad Boy South division and signed 8-Ball and MJG as its first act. Now he and Block were putting a group together called Boyz N Da Hood. Boyz N Da Hood consisted of Young Jeezy, Jody Breeze, Big Duke and Big Gee. I met Puff in passing on the set of Boyz N Da Hood's first music video

"Dem Boyz." But we met properly a few months later when Block had Puff fly me up to New York to discuss me signing to Bad Boy South.

Jeezy had dropped his debut album and become a superstar. He had started to distance himself from the group and Block and Puff were on the hunt for a new fourth member for Boyz N Da Hood. I was under consideration but Block was on the fence about it. He wasn't sure I'd be a good fit. Block really believed in me and viewed me in the same vein as a Biggie or a Jay-Z. I was an artist meant to stand on my own. He was leaning toward having Gorilla Zoe replace Jeezy. But he still wanted Puff to sign me.

Puff agreed with the sentiment that I was a down South Biggie. And that was the problem. That was the last thing he wanted. Puff had launched Bad Boy South to have a stake in the sound of the South. The game was changing and New York was losing its position as the dominant sound of hip-hop. So Puff wasn't looking for a rapper from the South that reminded people of the greatest East Coast lyricist that ever lived. That comparison alone was too much pressure for him.

I was getting desperate. Every now and then I think about all the times I've been asked whether or not I'm in the Illuminati. I can't help but laugh. Because back then, if all I had to do was sell my mind, body and soul in exchange for $100 million, I would have taken that deal in a heartbeat. I would have been reptilian as a motherfucker.

But there were no deals with the Devil. This was actually the first time I can remember turning to God to help me change my life. This was when Steve Smoke got me to take communion at the Calvary Chapel in Fort Lauderdale.

Steve Smoke was Duece's landlord. Duece was living at Alexander Towers, a fifteen-story oceanfront condo building in

Hollywood, Florida. Steve was a sixty-something-year-old white dude who owned close to a hundred of these apartments.

I liked Steve but he was a straight-up square. He would always come by the apartment to talk to Duece about back rent he owed or the smell of weed spilling out of the apartment into the hallway. As soon as Steve would get off the elevator you could hear him down the hall complaining about it.

"Ohhhhhh, Duece! It smells like a freaking skunk out here!"

Duece got away with being a bad tenant because Steve did other business with Ted at Slip-N-Slide. That was how Duece got hooked up with the condo in the first place. Through Steve's dealings with Slip-N-Slide, he'd heard about the new kid causing all sorts of problems at the label. Steve's nickname for me was "the heathen" and he would always ask about me.

Steve was a devout follower of Jesus Christ and an active member of the Calvary Chapel, an evangelical megachurch in Fort Lauderdale. As part of his Christian duties, Steve had been encouraged to go out and bring in new converts. When Steve would come over and see all the weed, guns and hoes he decided we were souls in need of saving.

"Duece, you have got to change your life," Steve said. "I want you to come to church with me on Sunday. If you can get the heathen to come with you, we can forget about last month's rent."

I had no interest in going but I owed Duece. My domestic violence case with Lastonia had gotten resolved by me agreeing to attend weekly anger management classes and Duece joined me for every one of them. Duece had no reason to be there but was the only one spilling his guts to the counselor about all the pimping and dope-selling he used to do and how it had traumatized him. Me and every other nigga in there were just going through the motions to get this over with but Duece loved therapy. He got me through those anger management classes so I had to return the favor and go to church with Steve Smoke.

Calvary Chapel hosted more than 20,000 worshippers every week. I had a little familiarity with megachurches—E-Class, Pucci and I used to ride around the city listening to Creflo Dollar's books on tape on prosperity theology—but to really be in one of these places was a spectacle. Unlike Creflo Dollar's World Changers Church, the Calvary Chapel's congregation was made up of all rich, white Florida people. The only black faces I can recall seeing in there were Donna Summer and her younger sister Mary Gaines Bernard, who were a part of the church choir. Pastor Bob Coy had founded Calvary Chapel after years of working in the music industry, so they had a mean musical presentation going on there.

I had gone to the Calvary Chapel as a favor to Duece and because Steve would always take us out to eat at Outback Steakhouse afterward. When it was time to take communion, Steve would always look back at us waiting for us to go up to the front. By that point Duece and I were usually ready to go smoke and get the fuck out of there. Steve would just shake his head.

But something kept me coming back. I would be sitting there in church and my phone would be blowing up in my pocket with all sorts of messages that could get me twenty-five-to-life. It got me thinking. Did I need to be saved? Were these messages the Devil leading me to temptation? After a few weeks of going to Sunday service I finally decided to take communion. I ate the wafer and drank the wine, praying that the blood of the lamb had washed away my sins. When I looked back at Steve Smoke there were tears in his eyes.

Maybe it was a coincidence but things actually started to turn around for me after that. I can't recall exactly when it was that I took communion but I do know it was November of 2005 when I got the phone call from Josh that changed my life.

"Can you slide through C.O.'s house?" he asked. C.O. was

another artist signed to Slip-N-Slide as part of the group Tre+6. "I've got this record here... Just come through ASAP."

Josh had gotten this beat CD from an A&R at Atlantic for consideration for Trick's next album. Not only had Trick already passed on this beat but supposedly T.I., Young Jeezy and Juelz Santana had too. But Josh thought this was going to be the one to turn everything around for me. It was produced by The Runners, a duo from Orlando. Josh loaded the CD up and pressed Play. It impacted me immediately.

EVERY DAY I'M HUSTLIN'... EVERY DAY I'M HUSTLIN'... EVERY DAY I'M HUSTLIN'...

Josh wasn't lying. This was a hit just off the hook alone. I didn't even need to write a chorus for this. As jaded as I was I couldn't deny what my ears were telling me. This beat felt like something. Josh and I sat in the studio listening to it for hours.

The next day we were headed up to Tampa, where I was opening for Trina. During the drive I had the instrumental playing on repeat. I lit up a joint, pulled out a pen and pad, and started writing. By the time we got to the venue I had a finished verse and I wanted to test it out. I took the CD out of the car and brought it inside.

At the end of my set I slipped the CD to Trina's DJ, Griot.

"I need you to play this track on here," I told him.

It's not easy for an opening act to grab the attention of the audience. Trust me on that. I did it a lot. These people were here to see Trina and I was someone they had to put up with to get there. But as soon as Griot pressed Play on "Hustlin'" I had them eating out of my palm. Then I went for it.

Who the fuck you think you fuckin' with? I'm the fuckin' BOSS
745, white on white, that's fuckin' ROSS
I cut 'em wide, I cut 'em long, I cut 'em fat

I keep 'em coming back, we keep 'em coming back
I'm into distribution, I'm like Atlantic
I got them motherfuckers flyin' across the Atlantic
I know Pablo, Noriega
The real Noriega, he owe me a hundred favors
I ain't petty nigga, we buy the whole thang
See most of my niggas really still deal cocaine
My roof back, my money right
I'm on the pedal, show you what I'm runnin' like
When they snatched Black I cried for a hundred nights
He got a hundred bodies, serving a hundred lifes

—"Hustlin',"
Port of Miami (2006)

The way the crowd responded to me that night was something I had never experienced. Nobody at this show had ever heard "Hustlin'." It wasn't even a song. I had written a verse to an instrumental in the van two hours earlier. Now, somehow, there were a thousand people in front of me screaming "Every day I'm hustlin'" in unison like it was a classic record they'd all heard a million times before.

There was this one guy in the crowd. He had on something dark green. I'll never forget the look he gave me that night. I'd never gotten one of those looks before. It was something different. Something powerful. My music had touched this motherfucker's soul. He hadn't just heard "Hustlin'" with his ears. It had hit him in his chest. I knew in that moment that whatever it was I had just tapped into with this song, that was where I needed to take my music going forward. I can still see his face so clearly.

Josh was smiling when I stepped offstage.

"I think we got one, Fatboy," he told me.

The next day I went to Poe Boy Studios and wrote two more

verses to "Hustlin'." After I laid down the track, Josh and I went
to go see Ted.

As fed up as I was with Slip-N-Slide, Ted was probably more
fed up with me. I wouldn't be surprised if he was trying to find
someone to take my contract off his hands like he'd taken me
off Draper's. I'd been shitting on him and his label personally
and publicly and now I was in his office trying to get him to
put a bag behind my record.

"You know Atlantic's not supporting him no more, right?"
Ted said. "So if we want to push this we've got to do it with
our own money. You believe in it that much?"

"Absolutely," Josh told him. "One hundred percent."

The following Friday, E-Class brought "Hustlin'" to 99 Jamz.
E-Class and Khaled were tight and that had helped smooth out
the friction between us. Khaled had been supporting my music
a little while before we brought him "Hustlin'." But he was really going to have to support this one, otherwise he could easily
end up back on my shit list. That wouldn't be an issue though.
Khaled didn't just play the record that night. He went above
and beyond his call of duty.

"This is that official brand-new Rick Ross! It's DJ Khaled!
It's 99 Jamz! It's Carol City! It's 305 M-I-YAYO!"

EVERY DAY I'M HUSTLIN'... EVERY DAY I'M HUSTLIN'...
EVERY DAY I'M HUSTLIN'...

Khaled didn't let the record ride for ten seconds before he
brought it back and started it from the top. And then he kept
bringing it back. This went on for maybe ten minutes before
he got to my verse.

Who the fuck you think you fuckin' with? I'm the fuckin' BOSS
745, white on white, that's fuckin' ROSS—

"Shout-out to E-Class! Poe Boy! Slip-N-Slide!"

And then he started it over. Khaled was going ape shit. He took a four-minute song and stretched it out over an hour, playing it back to back to back. He took the premiere of "Hustlin'" and turned it into something cinematic. That's when everything changed.

From the moment Khaled dropped the bombs on "Hustlin'" the Rick Ross movement became a full court press. The whole city got behind me. Anybody who didn't knew to get out of the way.

Khaled and every other radio DJ in Miami were playing the record to the point that they were getting in trouble with their program managers. Within weeks the same thing started happening in New York. Khaled had slipped the record to DJ Cipha Sounds, who was filling in for Funkmaster Flex at Hot 97 during the holidays. He kept dropping "Hustlin'" back to back until he got an email from Ebro, Hot 97's music director, asking him what the fuck he was doing playing an unknown artist's song on repeat. That was completely against protocol.

Greg Street got "Hustlin'" circulating too. He wasn't just getting my song played on V-103 in Atlanta. Greg was the cofounder of The Hittmenn DJs, a coalition of DJs that spanned thirty markets throughout the South and Midwest and reached millions of people.

The song was going crazy in the strip clubs too. I was seeing it for myself at places like Tootsie's, Coco's and Rollexx. But I kept hearing about this DJ that was burning "Hustlin'" at Diamonds. Diamonds Cabaret was the upscale spot where all the baddest bitches danced. It was a little uppity for my liking. They didn't let you wear shorts or smoke inside. So I'd never been.

But this mystery DJ had played "Hustlin'" so many times that he got himself suspended from the club. Then he came back and did it all over again and got himself fired. Nobody from my team had been slipping him money to play the song and he hadn't reached out to anyone.

People had been telling me about this DJ for weeks before I found out it was my little Haitian homie Sam Sneak. I'd met Sneak a few years back at another club called MVP. He was a skinny teenager who wasn't old enough to drink in the clubs he was spinning records at. I hadn't seen him in a while but he was out here showing me all this love and looking for nothing in return. The boy had heart. I appreciated it so much I made him my official DJ from that point on.

Meanwhile E-Class, Gucci Pucci and the rest of the Poe Boy street team—shout-out to Johnny Boy—had taken over the streets of Miami. Earlier I described E-Class as someone who can muscle his way into making things happen. That is most definitely true. But to leave it at that would be doing E a disservice. As "Hustlin'" was taking off E-Class found his true talent was in marketing and promotions. He seized the moment I was having and made it look larger than life.

There were Rick Ross posters on every corner of the city. E-Class bought a cherry picker to make sure mine stood heads above the others we were competing for eyeballs with. There were picket signs. T-shirts. Rick Ross hot air balloons. Water bottles. Ten-foot-tall cardboard cutouts. When NBA All-Star Weekend rolled around, E-Class put thirty of those motherfuckers on the side of a white diesel semi truck and drove that bitch all the way to Houston.

You couldn't go scuba diving in Miami without seeing my face. At one point E-Class found some waterproof material for boards and put them underwater. E was on some other shit. His whole strategy was genius.

Meanwhile Ted was setting up meetings with all the major labels. Every one of them had come calling. Even the donkeys at Atlantic, who pretended like they still had the first rights of refusal. As if I'd just forgotten how everything went down a year before. We had them come down to Miami and take us out to eat at Prime One Twelve on Ocean Drive. We'd ordered everything on the menu: crab cakes, crab legs, jumbo fried shrimp with watermelon, lobster mac-n-cheese, bone-in rib eyes and porterhouse steaks. Deep-fried Oreos and red velvet cake for dessert and a whole bunch of food to go. We maxed out their corporate credit cards.

Lyor Cohen was the president of Warner Music Group, the parent company of Warner Bros. Records and Atlantic Records, which had just merged. Lyor knew better than to send Craig and Mike back our way so he had Tom Whalley, the chairman and CEO of Warner Bros., try to bring me on board.

This bidding war was going down in the middle of the holidays, when the music industry usually shuts down for a few weeks. But this couldn't wait. Someone was going to sign Rick Ross. So Tom flew me, Ted, E-Class and Josh out to his big-ass mansion on Sunset Boulevard in Beverly Hills, where Tom and his team wined and dined us over a fancy dinner party. Even the chef and maids were trying to impress us. They made a whole show of it and I've got to give them credit, it was pretty damn impressive.

Whalley was a cool dude. Fifteen years earlier he'd signed a young Tupac Shakur to Interscope and A&R'ed his debut album, *2Pacalypse Now*. Kevin Liles, the executive vice president at WMG, and Lorenzo "Irv" Gotti were also at the dinner to close a deal with me. Irv Gotti was the founder of Murder Inc. Records. He had just been acquitted of money laundering charges that brought his company to its knees a year earlier. He was working with Lyor and Kevin to bring Murder Inc. back under Warner Bros., and signing me could signal the label's big comeback.

Right as we were boarding a flight back home, Ted got a

phone call. It was Shakir Stewart, the vice president of A&R for Def Jam Records.

"I just heard you're in California! Please don't sign that deal with Tom Whalley!"

"How the hell did you know we were out here?" Ted said.

"Everybody knows!" Shakir said.

"Listen, we haven't signed with anybody yet. We're just hearing everybody out. We're taking a red-eye back to Miami now."

"Okay, great," Shakir said. "When you land there will be a jet waiting for you. I'll see you guys in New York tomorrow morning."

Twelve hours later I was in a conference room at Def Jam's headquarters in Manhattan. Shakir made a strong first impression. He had come up to New York from Atlanta, where he was based, and I could tell he had his finger on the pulse of what was happening with hip-hop in the South. He was the A&R behind Def Jam signing Young Jeezy, whose debut album, *Thug Motivation 101*, was cranking out hit after hit. Shakir was on top of his shit.

I sensed the same from Def Jam's CEO, L.A. Reid, who said Shakir had played him my music while they were vacationing together in St. Tropez. L.A. Reid's expertise was more R&B than it was hip-hop—he'd just come to Def Jam after a legendary run with Babyface at La Face Records—but he seemed to understand and believe in what I was trying to do. I appreciated that he wasn't just an executive but had been an artist himself. This was not some out-of-touch label head trying to cash in on the success of one hit record.

I had a good feeling about these guys already. And then Jay-Z walked in the room.

Jay-Z said he'd known of me for a little while. His right-hand man Memphis Bleek had spoken to him about me prior to "Hustlin'" taking off. I'd met Bleek and State Property—a rap crew out of Philadelphia signed to Roc-A-Fella—a few years back at Circle House. Bleek was working with Trick Daddy on a record called "Round Here." But that day at Circle House we'd had a cypher and I'd battled the whole State Property crew for over an hour. Beanie Sigel, Freeway, The Young Gunz. I gave it to all them niggas. Apparently I'd made such an impression on them it had gotten back to Jay-Z.

Jay-Z and I had a connection we didn't speak of during that meeting. As a matter of fact, we have never spoken about it. But it has always been understood. It's the reason I have gotten more features from Jay-Z over the course of my career than any artist I can think of. It's the reason Jay-Z said, "Slip-N-Slide, Roc-A-Fella, One Umbrella" on the "Hustlin'" remix. It was because of Josh's big homie Versace Neal. Hov knew Neal from his former life and that relationship was what was behind all of my early work with Roc-A-Fella. My cyphers with Kanye at Studio Center. My battle with State Property at Circle House. My little cameo in the "Round Here" music video. All of these things were made possible because of a relationship that preceded music. And that made partnering with Jay-Z at Def Jam even more appealing to me. Do you know what I mean when I say this shit is deeper than rap?

All of the pieces were there. Def Jam already felt like home. But they were still going to have to come correct with the numbers because we already had a lot of big offers on the table. That's when Hov made his final pitch.

"I just came over here as president," he said. "And I want to close this deal but I'm not interested in doing much negotiating. So tell me what you need and if it's fair to you and it makes sense for Def Jam then I'll get it done."

"Seven figures," I told him.

"Done."

That was all she wrote. The Rick Ross bidding war was won.

CHAPTER

11

"HUSTLIN'" NOT ONLY CHANGED THE course of my career. It ushered in a new dawn for hip-hop in Miami. My success was immediately followed by my peers'. Khaled dropped back-to-back hits—"Holla at Me" and "Born-N-Raised"—that featured Pitbull, Trick Daddy and me, and were produced by Cool & Dre and The Runners. Speaking of Dre, my homie stepped out from behind the boards with a hit record of his own that I was featured on called "Chevy Ridin' High." Then I came back around and followed up "Hustlin'" with a *Scarface*-sampling second single called "Push It." Now everybody was eating. We called our collective success "The Movement" and none of us planned to slow down.

When I planted my flag on the roof of Club Rollexx for the "Hustlin'" music video, I felt like I'd taken over the world. But that triumphant feeling didn't last long. Soon the fear started to settle in. It had taken so long for me to get here and I had no idea how long the moment was going to last. I'd seen Luke go from having it all to losing it all and the thought of that happening to me was my worst nightmare. I'd be in a casket before I ended up on an episode of *Where Are They Now?*

The fear kept me focused. I wasn't going to let this success pass me by. There was so much pressure to follow "Hustlin'" with something even bigger and I wasn't going to crack under the pressure. So for the first nine months after I got my deal at Def Jam I didn't spend a dime of my advance. I didn't spend any of my show money either. I spent those nine months doing two things. Getting to the money on the road and getting in the studio to craft my debut album, *Port of Miami*.

I felt like I'd cracked the code with "Hustlin'." It wasn't that I'd gotten good at rapping all of a sudden. If anything, I'd dumbed down my lyrics on the song. I'd been rapping circles around my peers for damn near a decade. But I hadn't found the right production to match the message. On my mixtapes I was rapping over $500 beats or jacking industry instrumentals.

"Hustlin'" changed that. Producers heard the magic that I was capable of and started sending me quality beats that fit the formula. Production that captured the allure and mystique of South Beach with lyrics that spoke to the other side of the city across the bridge. That recipe became the driving force behind the sound of *Port of Miami*.

I was getting booked for so many shows. In the three months after "Hustlin'" dropped, my rate went from $5,000 to $15,000 to $25,000. That was a serious raise from the $250 shows I used to do, and I had no intentions of leaving any money on the table. Every bag had to be gotten. That meant that I had to make an album on the go.

During a stop in Orlando I met up with The Runners and grabbed three more beats from them. In Atlanta I recorded "Cross That Line" with Akon and "For Da Low" with Jazze

Pha. In New York I got in the studio with Jay-Z for the first time for the "Hustlin'" remix. In Los Angeles I met J.R. Rotem and took home the beat for "Push It."

I was pushing to the limit. I was on the road seven days a week, and on weekends I was doing up to three shows per night with helicopters taking me from one venue to the next.

It took a toll on me. My vocal cords were shot and my throat was killing me. I had doctors coming to my hotel room to give me vitamin B12 shots and I was sucking on ice cubes in the studio to get through those final *Port of Miami* sessions. At one point I was considering vocal cord surgery. You can hear how hoarse my voice had gotten all throughout the album. That wasn't some sound effect.

All in all, I cut about forty records over a ninety-day span. That collection of songs eventually got filtered down to a potent nineteen-song track list. It wasn't easy. But when *Port of Miami* finally dropped that August, my hard work proved to be worthwhile.

While the runaway success of 'Hustlin'' could have positioned Ross for one-hit-wonder status, he confidently sidesteps this fate by delivering the goods on Port of Miami. *With a cohesive sound the city can call its own, the bearded rapper gets the release he needs by exposing the dark side of the Sunshine State.*

—XXL

A blustery hip-hop antihero, barrel-size Miami rapper Rick Ross used his molasses-thick voice to tackle basically a single subject: cocaine. On Port of Miami, *Ross turns the minute details of drug distribution and dealing into ominous, slow-rolling songs, like the hypnotic, organ-driven hit single 'Hustlin'' and the Scarface-goes-South Beach stomp of 'Cross that Line.' In general, the whole 'crack rap' trend is a disheartening one, but Ross' pulpy debut manages to enthrall despite the drug-centric lyrics.*

—Entertainment Weekly

Bolstered by the hit single 'Hustlin',' Miami rapper Rick Ross' debut album Port of Miami *bows at the top of The Billboard 200. The Slip-N-Slide/Def Jam effort sold 187,000 copies in the United States last week, according to Nielsen SoundScan. Port of Miami also crowns the Top Rap Albums and Top R&B/Hip-Hop Albums tallies.*

—Billboard

Jay-Z called after the numbers came in. "Hustlin'" had already been certified platinum earlier that summer, in what was the first time an artist sold more than a million singles prior to releasing a debut album. Now I had the number one album in the country. *Port of Miami* had sold 187,000 copies in its first week.

"It's a 187, nigga!" Jay-Z shouted. "We killin' 'em!"

Jay-Z and I got to celebrate properly a few weeks later at the MTV Video Music Awards. He had his own personal runner bringing us glasses of Ace of Spades to our seats at Radio City Music Hall. As we toasted to *Port of Miami*'s success, Ludacris and Pharrell performed "Money Maker" on the stage in front of us. In that moment I realized how much of a gap there was in my success and Jay-Z's. Jay was relaxed. He was enjoying the award show and his bottle of champagne. I was enjoying myself too but that fear was still inside me. Jay-Z could never rap another bar for the rest of his life and he'd be straight. I wasn't there yet. I still had a lot further that I needed to go.

When *Port of Miami* went Gold in November I finally gave myself a moment to reset. It had been a full year of nonstop touring, recording and promoting my album. Weeks before I recorded "Hustlin'," my girlfriend Tia had given birth to our son William Leonard Roberts III. Lil Will. I was there for the delivery but I hadn't spent enough time with him since. I needed to fix that.

I was blessed to be a father again. Toie was the apple of my eye but I'd always wanted a son too. My relationship with Tia was a little more complicated. Tia and I had a good thing going for a while. If I was Biggie she most definitely resembled a young Faith Evans. But Tia could be a hot mess. Not only did she and I fight a lot but she would fight with my momma and sister too. She even got arrested one time for fighting Lastonia. Tia already had two boys of her own and a husband who was locked up in the feds so we were never going to work out long term. But I was trying to do the right thing and take care of her and Lil Will. I bought her a new Infiniti truck and made sure her rent and bills were paid for.

In December I bought myself a three-story, six-bedroom, seven-bathroom house in Fayetteville, Georgia. My first million-dollar home. As expected, Atlanta had become the epicenter of hip-hop and I wanted to be where business was booming. After I got settled I got to work on my next album, *Trilla*.

I wanted to do this album a little differently. *Port of Miami* was deeply rooted in my hometown. Now I wanted to go beyond the 305. The title alone was a tribute to my influences outside the city, combining Houston slang—"Trill"—and Michael Jackson's *Thriller*. I also wanted to take my time with it. Most of *Port of Miami* had been written in the back seat of a conversion van between tour stops. The end result was amazing but the creative conditions were far from ideal.

I must have taken too much time because by the end of 2007 Def Jam was starting to get impatient. It had been a year and a half since *Port of Miami* dropped and the label wanted to put some numbers on the board. We'd released a single called "Speedin'" but it didn't go over too well. "Speedin'" was actually a dope record and we shot a video for it where I was racing speedboats with Diddy and Fat Joe. The problem was I put R. Kelly on the record. R. Kelly had gotten indicted on charges of child pornography and with his court date looming I think a lot of radio stations were afraid to support "Speedin'" in case he was found guilty. If I knew all I know now I probably would not have put him on the song. But this was way before Twitter and social media and I was pretty naive to how sick he was.

I had another single with T-Pain that we all knew was going to be huge. But the label wanted to be able to drop *Trilla* on the heels of the single so the album needed to be done. *Trilla* had already gotten pushed back several times due to sample clearance issues and in that time Tony Draper had dropped *Rise to Power*, a collection of years-old unreleased material from my days at Suave House. Draper compensated me for that but Def Jam wasn't too happy.

I was ready to turn in *Trilla* too. But it was still missing something. Jay-Z hadn't sent in his vocals. Hov had blessed me with a verse for the "Hustlin'" remix but I wanted us to have a proper song of our own. Jay-Z had stepped down from his position as Def Jam president so he wasn't working on their schedule. But he wasn't going to let me down either. At the eleventh hour, he came through.

Josh flew up to New York and met up with Jay-Z and Shakir at Battery Studios. That's when he played Hov "Maybach Music." I'd gotten the beat from J.U.S.T.I.C.E. League, a production team from Tampa. As soon as I heard the beat I knew I wanted to get Jay on it. And I knew I wanted the song to be called "Maybach Music." What first started as a concept for a song would go on to become a six-part series and the name of my record label. Now it's synonymous with everything I do. When you think Maybach, you think Ricky Rozay.

The Mercedes-Benz Maybach had just beaten out Rolls-Royce and Bentley as the world's most prestigious automobile according to the Luxury Brand Status Index. I didn't know too much about that list but I did know the Maybach was the ultimate symbol of prestige.

I've most definitely purchased a few Maybach coupes in my day—a 57S and the S650 Cabriolet—but the back of a Maybach 62 is where you want to be. That's the elongated sedan with reclining rear seats and more legroom than you know what to do with. It's got TV screens embedded in the back of the front seats. Writing desks that unfold from the armrests like in a plane. The back seat is where it's at. Because the truth is a Maybach is not a car you purchase to drive. It's a car to be chauffeured in.

In my imagination the Maybach became a symbol of the quality of music I wanted to make. It represented the amount of time and attention to detail it took to make something special. Music that sounded so exclusive and luxurious that someone could put it on in their hoopty and feel like they were just transported to the back of a 62S.

The beat for "Maybach Music" sampled a cover of an old Beatles record so J.U.S.T.I.C.E. League had to re-create the sample five times before Sony ATV and Paul McCartney allowed us to put it out. Then they added live instrumentation on top of the sample. The meticulousness that went into making "Maybach Music" embodied the whole concept behind it.

When Josh got back from New York he told me Hov freestyled his "Maybach Music" verse in one take just like I'd seen him do when we recorded the remix to "Hustlin'." He also said Hov had given us a little something extra to go with his verse. These two Australian supermodels—shout-out to Jessica Gomes and Cheyenne Tozzi—had been hanging out at the studio while he was recording and they had some sexy accents. Hov sent them into the booth and told them to talk that Maybach talk.

"What is this?"

"Maybach Music."

"I like this Maybach Music."

"Sweeeeet..."

Then they both laughed. And that's how the iconic "Maybach Music" drop was born. It's been over ten years since that studio session and I'm still not sick of hearing it. There's something timeless about the exchange. Jay-Z said something funny to me about it a few years later. By then I was dropping it in every song I put out. I started laughing when he said it. Hov doesn't forget anything.

I'm still waiting for you to thank me for that.

CHAPTER

12

Photo by Julia Beverly.

Photo by Julia Beverly.

Photo by Julia Beverly.

Photo by Julia Beverly.

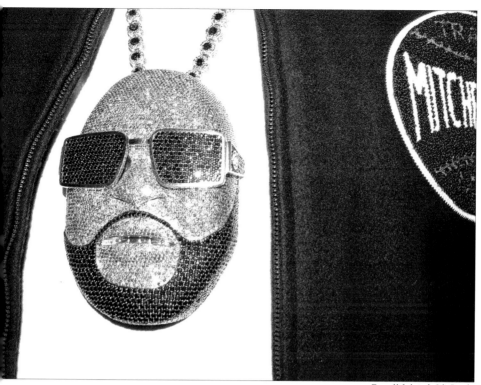

Top and left photos by Julia Beverly.

Photo by Shareif Ziyadat/FilmMagic/Getty Images.

Photo by Julia Beverly.

Photo by C Brandon/Redferns/Getty Images.

Photo by Johnny Nunez/Getty Images.

Photo by Donaldson Collection/Getty Images.

Photo by Kevin Mazur/Getty Images.

Photo by Prince Williams/Getty Images.

Photo by Prince Williams/Getty Images.

Photo by Julia Beverly.

Photo by Julia Beverly.

Photo by wowcelebritytv/Bauer-Griffin/Getty Images.

Photo by CBS Photo Archive/Getty Images.

Photo by Prince Williams/Getty Images.

I HAVE THE GIFT OF FORESIGHT. I CAN SEE
the different ways that a situation might play out. Every possible outcome. But not every time. There are some storms you
never see coming.

There would be no sophomore slump. *Trilla* was another number one, selling just shy of 200,000 copies in its first week. "The
Boss," my single with T-Pain, landed in the Top 20 of the Billboard Hot 100, becoming my second certified platinum record
after "Hustlin'."

Things were going pretty good. The label was happy. The
fans were happy. The money was piling up. I was dating Foxy
Brown and that relationship was exciting. I'd had a thing for
Foxy since I first heard her on a song called "Touch Me, Tease
Me" back in '96. I met her on the set of DJ Khaled's video for
"Out Here Grinding" that summer and we hit it off.

Aside from a minor legal issue I didn't have much to complain about. At the top of 2008 I'd gotten arrested in North Miami after a traffic stop. I'd been charged with carrying a concealed weapon and possession of marijuana. The arrest was nothing to be too worried about. The weed charge had already gotten dropped and soon the gun one would be too. I had a license to carry but due to an error, my permit had registered as suspended.

The case was going to get dismissed. The only part that was concerning was when my lawyer found out my case had been assigned to the police department's gang task force. During a deposition of the arresting officer, he was told it was because of my alleged ties to a gang called the Carol City Cartel.

"Why was this case assigned to the gang task force?"

"Because your client claims affiliation with the Carol City Cartel and other known gang members."

"Where did you get that from?"

"Other detectives."

"Is that pulled out of the vast universe, or do you have something definitive?"

"I think there is some literature or video on YouTube that you can pull up for yourself."

I had to move with a little more caution. I'd worn a "Boobie Boys" T-shirt in the "Hustlin'" video. Then I put out a documentary called *M-I-Yayo* counting down the Top 10 dope boys in Miami history. I was essentially taunting law enforcement.

I was still too connected to the streets to be acting so reckless. So I was being mindful of my moves around this time. I was aware that something from my past could get dug up and used against me. It just never occurred to me that it could be the thing it ended up being.

Halfway through the summer I got a call from one of my homies telling me there was something I needed to see. A website had published a photograph of me at a graduation ceremony for the Florida Department of Corrections. I was dressed in a

correctional officer uniform and shaking hands with a middle-
aged white lady by the name of Marta Villacorta. Marta was the
warden for the South Florida Reception Center, a state prison
in Doral.

The article said the picture confirmed rumors that I had once
worked as a correctional officer. The subtext was this made me
a fraud. That all my talk about moving kilos in my raps were
lies if this were true. Immediately the story started to spread
like wildfire.

Report: Rick Ross Worked as a Florida Corrections Officer

—Rolling Stone

Rick Ross Correction Officer Rumor Confirmed

—XXL

Rick Ross's Coke-Rap Career Imperiled by Charges of Law Enforcement

—Vulture

I'm talking about this here—as opposed to earlier in the book
when it took place—because this is when my time as a correctional officer became an important part of my story. Prior to
this moment I'd thought of it no differently than when I used
to wash cars or when my momma got me a job for the Department of Health delivering medicine to people who were too
sick to leave their house.

When I dropped out of Albany State and moved home I
needed to get a job. I was getting money so it wasn't that I
needed the income so much as that I needed something to tell
my momma I was doing with my life. If I wasn't in college then
I had to get a job. Those were the rules if I wanted to live in
her house.

The job I really wanted was to work at the docks. I wanted to be a longshoreman. I used to bug Gino, my tattoo artist and good friend, to connect me with his younger brother Kano. Kano was part of a crew of Haitians called the R.O.C., which stood for "Rich Off Cocaine." They were known for pulling huge heists at the Port of Miami. They'd get tipped off about incoming cargo ships that were smuggling in some kilos and from there it could go one of two ways. Either Kano and his crew would highjack the freighters at sea, where they'd strip everybody naked, toss their phones into the ocean and get somebody to give up the goods. Or they would wait until the loads came off the docks. Then, disguised as undercover police officers, Kano and his crew would pull the smugglers over and rob them. They'd be in unmarked Crown Victorias outfitted with strobe lights and everything. This was high-level piracy.

I wanted to be the inside man at the docks but you needed a plug at the union to get that job. I would drop hints to Gino to get him to introduce me to Kano. In addition to tattoos, Gino did custom airbrushing and one afternoon I brought in a pair of Timberlands and $200 and told him I wanted him to write "Rich Off Cocaine" on them. The boots came out incredible but Gino didn't take the bait/bribe as far as connecting me with Kano. He didn't want to see either of us get into any more trouble than we were already getting into.

That's when I applied for a job at the Florida Department of Corrections. I already knew several niggas who worked as correctional officers. It was a common job for big mean former football players. It was also an easy job to get, because Florida has one of the highest incarceration rates in the country. Being a CO is not a job that someone with lifelong aspirations to work in law enforcement takes.

My first six months were spent in the Department of Corrections' basic recruit training program. The 540-hour course consisted of me taking multiple-choice tests, completing obstacle courses and learning first aid and CPR.

The main campus of the South Florida Reception Center is a violent place but they don't throw you to the wolves right away. As a Level I correctional officer I was assigned to a watchtower post in the prison's South Unit. The South Unit housed six hundred inmates, most of whom were either elderly or ill. After a few months in the tower I was promoted, which meant I got to escort these guys to the medical ward and stand by while they recovered from various surgeries and procedures. As you can imagine, these inmates didn't tend to cause many problems.

The play was to get transferred over to the main unit. Once I got over there this correctional officer shit was going to be a lick. The pay was still shit—my starting salary was less than $25,000—but this was where you could make money off the books by bringing in weed or letting niggas finger their girls during visitation. The main unit is where I would encounter niggas I knew. Or niggas that Mike or Boobie knew. Both of them had a lot of connections and influence in the correctional system. Really they had connections everywhere. The fire department. The phone company. The police.

For a while I made an effort to perform the job to the best of my ability. I showed up on time. I logged my hours. I wrote up the reports. But that didn't last too long. The thing people don't understand about prison, whether you're in there as an inmate or a CO, is how uneventful it is most of the time. I'd never been so bored in my life. I started smoking weed before I went in. Then I'd just sit there waiting for the days to be over. I'd look out past the barbed wire fence and imagine a different life waiting for me on the other side. Something better than this. Something special.

I never made it to the main unit. I think word may have gotten around to some of the higher-ups that I knew people over there. My supervisors weren't interested in transferring me over to the main campus and once I realized that wasn't happening I came to the conclusion that the job had run its course. So I quit. That was pretty much it.

But the blogs were spinning this story like I was an undercover cop or confidential informant. I couldn't believe it. The attack on my character caught me completely off guard.

There were plenty of people who had known about this. I'd never made an effort to cover it up. I used to pick up Gunplay after work to go to Earl's studio and I'd still be in my uniform. If anything, Gunplay was jealous his rap sheet prevented him from getting a government job with benefits. I think he was still working at the AT&T store at the time.

Anyone who was close enough to me to know about this would know better than to call my credibility into question. No girl had ever denied me pussy and no nigga had ever stepped on my toes over me being a correctional officer. Because the moment anyone got close enough to smell the cloth that I was cut from, they knew that I was trained to go.

This had to be coming from somebody who was close enough to know the truth but wanted to sabotage me anyway. And the public didn't know any better than to believe whatever story the websites were feeding them. Before I had a chance to address the situation myself one of the blogs put out a story with a statement from me denying the authenticity of the photo.

"My life is 100% real. These online hackers putting a picture of my face when I was a teenager in high school on other people's body. If this shit was real, don't you think they would have more specifics, like dates and everything?"

I hadn't said that. I hadn't spoken to any outlet about the situation. I don't know if they made up the quote or if somebody from my camp issued it on my behalf. But it didn't come from me. What I do know is that those sites ending up taking those articles down. They didn't stand by their reporting.

But that part doesn't even matter because this is the moment where I made my mistake. Instead of setting the record straight then and there, I went and repeated the denial in interviews in the following days. The situation had unraveled so fast and I'd been made to feel like I had something to hide. Everything had been going so well and now everybody was saying that I'd been exposed and my whole career was in jeopardy. I'd never seen a meme in my life and all of a sudden I was seeing these pictures of my head photoshopped onto the movie posters for *RoboCop* and *Big Momma's House*.

I should have taken a minute to assess the situation and respond appropriately. Instead I got caught up in the drama and reacted hastily. When another website site dug up my personnel file a week later, it made everything way worse. Now I wasn't just being called an imposter. I was a liar too. And that part was actually true. I had no one to blame for that but myself. The worst thing about a lie is once you've put it out there you've got to dig your heels into it and keep it up. And for a while that's what I did.

The whole rap game was in a frenzy over whether or not Rick Ross was a fraud. Everybody had an opinion. Maino said he was disappointed in me. Ludacris, Fabolous and Fat Joe came to my defense. Even Freeway Rick came out of the woodwork to say I'd stolen his identity.

I was fuming. Even toward the people who knew what it was and were in my corner. Because why the fuck were these niggas even being asked to weigh in on this in the first place? The situation woke me up to the power of the blogs and the ways that they keep a story going. I was being used as clickbait. Money was being made at the expense of my livelihood.

My frustrations boiled over at the 2008 Ozone Awards in

Houston. *Trilla* won Album of the Year that night but I couldn't even enjoy it. I was in war mode. When my crew ran into DJ Vlad, one of the bloggers who had been pouring gasoline on the fire, he took a beating on behalf of everybody who had been out there throwing dirt on my name. Broken nose. Broken eye socket. Seven stitches. The incident would cost me $300,000 in a settlement. I think all parties involved learned the cost of doing business that night.

I would never say it out loud but I was in something of a dark place. The energy around me had gotten tense and it put a strain on my relationships. My fling with Foxy fizzled out. I had a falling out with E-Class and fired him as my manager. I severed all ties with Slip-N-Slide again.

Those weren't the only people that left my inner circle that year. In November I received a phone call telling me that Shakir Stewart had committed suicide. He'd shot himself in his Georgia home, leaving behind a fiancée and two kids. He was thirty-four years old.

I couldn't believe it. And I didn't even know what to believe. There were so many crazy rumors going around. That Shakir had been murdered. That he had been living a double life. It fucked me up.

With Shakir gone I didn't know what my future at Def Jam would look like. Jay-Z had resigned from his position as president of the label the year before. As much as I liked and respected L.A. Reid, his support and guidance was never hands-on like Shakir's was. Shakir had been the glue that held everything together. Whenever Ted and I weren't seeing eye-to-eye he would be the one to intervene and smooth things over. He was the best A&R I'd ever worked with. He had a rare gift of being able to connect the sound of the streets with the mainstream. That wasn't going to be easy to replace.

CHAPTER
13

THE WEEK THAT *TRILLA* CAME OUT WAS

the first time I heard my name come out of 50 Cent's mouth.

50 was beefing with Fat Joe at the time and he put out a video shitting on the low first-week sales of Joe's new album *The Elephant in the Room*.

"That's when you know you're not relevant. When you got new artists like Ricky Ross the Boss coming out looking real good with a number one album. He's from that same little pocket out there in Miami, but he shouldn't stand next to that fat piece of shit cause you know how I get. You know how I get, right?"

50 wasn't showing his hand just yet but I knew a veiled threat when I heard one. This was his MO. For years 50 had been starting beefs with rappers and then going after whoever stood by them. And it had worked. He'd crushed every adversary to date. 50 had already used his feud with Fat Joe as a way to start dissing Khaled. He was keeping it cordial with me for now, con-

gratulating me on *Trilla*'s success, but I knew if he was going after Khaled then it was only a matter of time before he came for me. 50 was just going down the line.

I didn't get back to 50 until the top of 2009. Coming off the correctional officer controversy, the last thing people around me wanted was a war with 50 Cent. We had enough problems already and 50 would have all the ammo he needed. I was told it would be self-sabotage.

But I viewed the situation differently. For six months I'd been on the defensive. For every DJ Vlad that got his wig split some other donkey would pop up in his place. I was playing *Whac-A-Mole*. But 50 Cent was a different story. This was the biggest bully in the rap game. If I sat his ass down then that would silence all the naysayers. It would be cutting the head off the snake.

I put 50 on notice with a few bars on a song called "Mafia Music," where I touched on recent reports that he had tried to burn his house down in the midst of a child support battle with his ex-girlfriend.

I love to pay your bills, can't wait to pay ya rent
Curtis Jackson baby mama, I ain't askin' for a cent
Burn the house down, nigga, you gotta buy another
Don't forget the gas can, jealous stupid motherfucker

—"Mafia Music,"
Deeper than Rap (2009)

"Really?" Khaled said when he first heard "Mafia Music." "This is how we're coming?"

Khaled had just been named president of Def Jam South and taken on Shakir's former role as my A&R and point person at the label. While he appreciated me coming to his defense, this was not how he wanted to kick things off the first week at his

new job. Khaled is a man of peace. "Mafia Music" was a dec-
laration of war.

50 fired back a few days later with "Officer Ricky." This
donkey had some nerve calling my credibility into question.
His whole career was based around him getting shot nine times.
Where I came from, getting shot was not something to be glo-
rified. We were the niggas doing the shooting.

50 was so fugazi. He had never gotten anywhere close to
the level I was at in the streets. The niggas he came up under
in Queens? They were the type of niggas I was giving bricks
to on consignment when I was eighteen and they were paying
me back every dime ahead of schedule. 50 wasn't even that. He
would have been the nigga I had filling my truck up with gas
before I went out of town. 50 Cent would have been buying
me air fresheners.

But I knew 50 would go the route that he did. It was the eas-
iest path in front of him. The part that surprised me was how
weak the song was. "Mafia Music" wasn't just me sending a few
lazy shots 50's way. It was some of my best rapping to date. No
chorus. Just four and a half minutes of straight bars. So I was
expecting the 50 Cent that ruined Ja Rule's career on "Back
Down." But "Officer Ricky" sounded like "Candy Shop" 2.0.
The song was fucking terrible.

"Yeah, I heard it," I told Angela Yee in a radio interview
with Shade 45 the next day. "I was positive that couldn't be the
response. Tell me he's joking. We're all gonna act like we ain't
hear that garbage. We're gonna give you another forty-eight
hours. Take your time. Go back in the lab and come up with
something else."

50 realized he couldn't compete with me bar for bar so he
switched up his strategy. He pivoted away from the music and
started coming at me through a strange series of publicity stunts.
There were "Officer Ricky" cartoons. Sketch-comedy videos

where he had on a curly perm wig. I thought I was hallucinating the first time I saw him with that shit on. This nigga was ocky!

I must have gotten under 50's skin by mentioning his problems with his baby momma because he started running with that theme. I wasn't burning my house down but I didn't have the cleanest yard myself. I was in the middle of my own custody dispute. I'd just gotten deposed in Broward County family court. 50 pounced on that. He got a hold of Tia and paid her a couple dollars to go out and trash me in interviews. Then he bankrolled her so she could put out a tell-all book about our relationship.

50 had his own book in the works at the time. He was writing one with Robert Greene, the author of *The 48 Laws of Power*. I'd read Greene's book and I didn't subscribe to all its teachings. I didn't support taking credit for other people's work or finding a scapegoat to blame for fuckups or posing as a friend to enemies. But I was most definitely putting a few of its principles into practice. Strike the shepherd and the sheep will scatter. Stir up waters to catch fish. Disarm and infuriate with the mirror effect. And crush your enemy totally.

48 Laws flawed, my dawgs above the law
Duck-tape Robert Greene, make him read the Quran

—"Wuzzup,"
Hood Billionaire (2014)

After he got everything he could out of Tia, 50 somehow came into possession of a sex tape of Lastonia and leaked it online. I can't say I was totally surprised. Lastonia was my homegirl but she got herself into situations like that. The only part that really bothered me was that it was going to affect Toie. I wanted to protect her and Lil Will from all of this. When 50 started posting pictures of him, Tia and Will together at Floyd Mayweather's house, a line had been crossed.

They say desperate people do desperate things and 50 seemed to get desperate quick. Once I saw that he was feeling the pressure and had to resort to doing all this gooky weirdo shit—the fucking donkey was stalking Khaled's mother at one point—I started to loosen up. I'd been on the defensive for so long that I'd forgotten how much I enjoyed putting the squeeze on a nigga. That's when I became the aggressor.

This is around the time I started shooting a lot of visuals with my videographer Spiff TV. We shot one for "Mafia Music" and right after we went up to New York and did another one for a follow-up dis called "Kiss My Pinky Ring Curly." I wanted people to see what a square 50 was and that I was more certified in his city than he was. Torch had the Bronx behind me. Kano had Brooklyn behind me. 50 could *never* come to Miami like that.

Then I recruited Game, Ja Rule and Fat Joe—who had all had their own problems with Curly—to get on a remix to "Mafia Music" and get their jabs in. Then I held a mock funeral for 50 in the music video for "In Cold Blood."

Family over the money, money over the bitches
Money don't mean nothin', then why they callin' it riches
I'm addicted to watches, Mama tellin' me stop it
Got one over on 50, 50 you better watch it

—"In Cold Blood,"
Deeper than Rap (2009)

Spiff was ahead of his time when it came to shooting videos with DSLR cameras. We started posting new content to WorldStarHipHop every other day and rappers were coming up to me asking how I got Def Jam to cut the check for all these music videos and vlogs. But the label hadn't put up a penny for those. It was just Spiff shooting them guerilla style on the fly. Soon every rapper had a shooter following them with a Canon 5D.

Meanwhile 50 kept spending all his money. I don't know how much he put into Tia's book but that sex tape with Lastonia would cost him $5 million in an invasion-of-privacy lawsuit. I was getting approached by people claiming to have all types of dirt on 50 and G-Unit but I just couldn't bring myself to pay money for some gossip. So I just kept my foot on his neck with the music and the vlogs, clowning him for how he dressed and his ugly-ass fake teeth.

Things had been tense for so long but at some point it started to get fun. I was a student of hip-hop. It was exciting to be a part of a rivalry like this and have the whole game in a frenzy. I even tried to up the ante by calling out 50's big homie Eminem but Em didn't take the bait.

50 started to quiet down after his album got pushed back. He had been trying to re-create the sales showdown that he'd had with Kanye West a year earlier. He'd spent all this money and time trying to take me out with the hope that it would revive his failing career and build hype for his album. The problem was putting out sex tapes and taking pictures with my son wasn't making his music any better. Every single he tried to put out was a dud. Interscope had already dropped Lloyd Banks and Tony Yayo, and 50 needed to go back to the drawing board if he wanted his label to give him a release date.

The whole time Woodface and I were going back and forth, I had an ace up my sleeve. I had something that 50's money couldn't buy him. It wasn't a dossier with all his dirty laundry. What I had waiting in the wings was a classic album. When my back was against the wall I'd made the best music of my career. And I was going to drop it when the pressure was at an all-time high and the lights were shining brightest. That's when I put the final nail in Curly's coffin. That's when I dropped *Deeper than Rap*.

In 2006, for the since-shuttered Blender, *I wrote about Ross' debut,* Port of Miami: *'[Ross] tends to sit on top of beats, insisting that his presence is enough to make a hit. It isn't.' Ross' smoky groan made him distinctive, but it was also a liability. When he began to slide into pocket last year, harnessing a surprisingly fluid flow and an impressive array of clever punchlines, questions about his past lingered—but they never overwhelmed. His progress manifests itself in surprising, and even thrilling ways on* Deeper Than Rap, *his third album and easily his best.*

—VIBE

His songs aimed at 50 Cent have, hands down, been sharper and wittier than those of his rival. And the just-released Deeper Than Rap, *his third album, is unexpectedly fantastic, by far his best.*

—The New York Times

Phony or not, Ross has planted himself near the center of hip-hop's orbit, and Deeper Than Rap *proves that it's going to take more than YouTube beefs and blogger scandal-mongering to move him out of the way.*

—SLANT Magazine

CHAPTER

14

TO BORROW THE WORDS OF MY BROTHER
DJ Khaled, *Deeper than Rap* was "Another One." But this victory was especially sweet. My third number one album had come in the face of adversity. I'd taken my licks but I'd come out the other side on top. When the chips were down and the odds were stacked against me I didn't curl up in a ball and hide. I stood tall and fought. Now everybody who counted me out had to eat their words.

I felt bulletproof. That feeling inspired a return to my former moniker for the title of my fourth album. *Teflon Don*. But before I could get started on that I needed to bring out my brothers who were with me back when I was Tef. I needed to introduce the world to Triple C's.

The group had been on the back burner since my solo career took off, but with the success of *Deeper than Rap* I finally felt secure in my future. Nobody was getting me out of here.

Gunplay and Torch had been waving the Triple C's flag in my absence and doing shows as a duo. But the identity of Triple C's was a three-headed monster. I wanted to get back to making music with Gunplay and Torch but I didn't want to leave them hanging when I got back to focusing on my own shit. I wanted Triple C's to be able to stand on its own without me. That's when I added Young Breed to the group.

Breed was ten years younger than me but his older brothers were street niggas I knew growing up. Even though he was a youngster, Breed had been rapping for a minute and people knew him in Miami. He was already in another group called Piccolo but he had been getting in the studio with Gunplay and Torch, who both spoke highly for him. The more I found out about Breed the more I thought he would be a good fit for Triple C's. He was the image that came to mind when you spoke the words *Carol City Cartel*. Whereas Torch was from the Bronx and Gunplay was this coked-up concoction of Miami, New York, Jamaica and Puerto Rico, Breed was a straight-up gutter Carol City nigga with dreads and golds rapping about Chevys and choppers.

I also wanted Triple C's to have its own representation outside of my management. So I promoted Geter K from muscle to manager. Geter was one of Torch's homies from the Bronx and he'd earned his keep hanging around us. Geter was a gladiator. He was the one who damn near punched Vlad's eye out of his head at the Ozone Awards. That wasn't the only time Geter's hands caused me a lawsuit but Triple C's was a rough-and-tumble crew that needed a militant manager. Geter fit the bill.

I'd just delivered three consecutive number one albums, so Def Jam was giving me what I wanted. And what I wanted was to have my own imprint, Maybach Music Group, and for its first release to be a Triple C's group album called *Custom Cars & Cycles*.

We had some much fun making *Custom Cars & Cycles* so it was disappointing when the album flopped. It was a period of transition at Def Jam following Jay-Z's exit and Shakir's passing, and the release slipped through the cracks. That was a shame because the album came out hard and people seemed to fuck with the group. It wasn't that people didn't like Triple C's. The album just wasn't promoted properly. Regardless I felt like I'd accomplished what I set out to do. I'd shined the light on my brothers and put them in a position to win.

I still had one more old friend I needed to help out before I could get started on *Teflon Don*. At the top of 2010 I received a call from Kanye West's management asking me to come to Hawaii. Kanye was holed up at Avex Honolulu Studios working on something. He'd booked all three of the studio's recording rooms for twenty-four hours a day until further notice.

Kanye had come to Hawaii to get away. It was his escape from his problems at home. A year and a half earlier he'd found refuge there following the loss of his mother. That retreat inspired his fourth album, *808s and Heartbreak*. This time around Kanye had come to Hawaii after a situation at the 2009 MTV Video Music Awards. He'd interrupted Taylor Swift's acceptance speech to say the award should have gone to Beyoncé. He got a lot of backlash for that. Even President Obama called him a jackass.

It had been eight years since I last saw Kanye. I'd gotten him on "Maybach Music 2" but that was done remotely. We hadn't actually been in a studio together since our cyphers at Studio Center back in 2002. A lot had changed since then. For both of us.

I wasn't sure what to expect of our reunion when me, Pucci

and Spiff checked into our Hilton hotel on Waikiki Beach. But once we got to the studio I started to gather that this wasn't going to be my typical guest verse. The first thing I noticed were all these signs Kanye had put up on the walls.

NO TWEETING
NO HIPSTER HATS
ALL LAPTOPS ON MUTE
JUST SHUT THE FUCK UP SOMETIMES
NO TWEETING PLEASE THANK YOU
NO BLOGGING
NO NEGATIVE BLOG VIEWING
DON'T TELL ANYONE ANYTHING ABOUT ANY-
THING WE'RE DOING!
NO RACKING FOCUS WHILE MUSIC IS BEING
PLAYED OR MUSIC IS BEING MADE
TOTAL FOCUS ON THIS PROJECT IN ALL STUDIOS
NO ACOUSTIC GUITAR IN THE STUDIO
NO PICTURES

I wasn't sure what tweeting was but I did know that something different was taking place here. Kanye had flown in a murderer's row of emcees, producers and songwriters to work on this project. Legendary beatmakers like No I.D., Pete Rock and DJ Toomp. Young superstars in the making like Nicki Minaj, Kid Cudi and Big Sean.

This was the routine. Every day would start at 10:00 a.m. with breakfast at Kanye's crib in Diamond Head. Sometimes we'd get there before he did. Kanye would still be at the studio from the night before. He had two full-time chefs there who were cooking up French toast with flambéed banana while everybody got to talking about what we'd worked on the night before and what we were fitting to do at the studio today. These were Knights of the Round Table discussions.

It was during one of those breakfasts that Kanye and I got to talking about Pusha T. Pusha was one half of the Virginia rap duo Clipse, who had just dropped their third album *Till the Casket Drops*. Kanye had been featured on the album on a song called "Kinda Like a Big Deal" but he never actually worked on the record. He'd recorded his verse on there for a T.I. song called "On Top of the World," but somehow it had ended up getting placed on the Clipse song instead.

So Kanye didn't know Pusha T. But I did and I gave Ye my opinion on him. Somebody like Pusha T could be a big asset in this environment and I recommended Kanye see what his label situation was too. I got them on the phone and the rest is history. I had already left Hawaii by the time Pusha got there but he got a few placements on the album and Kanye ended up signing him to G.O.O.D. Music.

After breakfast Kanye would go play a few games of pickup basketball at the YMCA. Spiff and I usually skipped out on the gym. We'd hop in our little Kia rental car and explore the island. We'd go to lunch at Benihana, and do some shopping. Spiff and I are toy collectors and we found a dope-ass toy store one day and bought mad shit.

Playtime was over at 3:00 p.m. That's when everyone would reconvene at the studio. For the next twelve hours it was all business.

Kanye's creative process was a little chaotic. He's a real theory. One minute Kanye would be with me working on "Live Fast, Die Young" and then suddenly he'd leave to see how Nicki's verse was coming along on "Monster" in the other room.

Nicki Minaj earned my respect as a lyricist that day. I knew she was Lil Wayne's protégé and had a big personality, but when I saw her sit down and write her verse on "Monster" from scratch, I was blown away. The girl was a superstar and she was setting it off on this record. I convinced Kanye to let me whip up a little four-bar bridge that we could squeeze between the song's intro and Kanye's hook.

> Bitch, I'm a monster, no good blood sucker
> Fat motherfucker, now look who's in trouble
> As you run through my jungles all you hear is rumbles
> Kanye West samples, here's one for example

—"Monster,"
My Beautiful Dark Twisted Fantasy (2010)

The next thing I knew I was in a closet with this cool bearded white brother getting ready to record. I'd seen this guy working out of this tiny room in the back. He'd been there since I got there. I figured he must be a stand-in for Mike Dean—Kanye's main engineer who hadn't gotten to Hawaii yet—but it turned out he was the voice behind the distorted vocals on the song's intro. We ended up smoking a whole bunch of joints and kicking the shit while I laid down my little verse.

This hippy motherfucker ended up being Justin Vernon of the band Bon Iver. But I didn't find that out until later. During the time we spent working together I had no clue who he was and I didn't think to ask. I had no doubt that anybody Kanye had flown down here was here for a good reason.

My biggest contribution to *My Beautiful Dark Twisted Fantasy* came several months after my trip to Hawaii. Kanye had to turn in his album the next day. But he wanted to get me on "Devil in a New Dress."

I'd already recorded a verse to "Devil in a New Dress" in Hawaii. It was a real soulful joint built around an old Smokey Robinson. Kanye had already released the song as part of his weekly G.O.O.D. Fridays series. Except he hadn't kept my verse on there. But when I met up with Kanye in New York at the final hour of his album he had a new version of the song. His engineer Mike Dean had added this mean guitar solo break-down at the end of it that Kanye wanted me to come in after. But he wanted me to write a new verse. He didn't like the one I'd done in Hawaii.

"I know that you can do something better than that," he told me.

That's what he said. Then he stood up, turned around and walked out the studio.

It was good that he left. I needed a minute to process what had just happened. In all my years no one had ever asked me to rewrite a verse before. Even when I was a nobody ghostwrit-ing for artists way bigger than me no one had ever said some-thing like that.

I was shocked but I wasn't offended. I wasn't pissed. That surprised me too. I knew Kanye hadn't said that to upset me. He was pushing me the same way he had been pushing every-body in Hawaii. The same way he was pushing himself to do something even greater. So the ball was in my court. I could either take his request as disrespect or I could take him up on his challenge. I decided on the latter and two hours later I had another verse. It's one that many of my fans consider to be the best of my career.

Lookin' at my bitch, I bet she give your ass a bone
Lookin' at my wrist, it'll turn your ass to stone
Stretch limousine, sippin' rosé all alone
Double-headed monster with a mind of his own
Cherry red chariot, excess is just my character
All black tux, nigga shoes lavender
I never needed acceptance from all you outsiders

Had cyphers with Yeezy before his mouth wired
Before his jaw shattered, climbing up the Lord's ladder
We still speeding, running signs like they don't matter
Hater talking never made me mad
Never that when I'm in my favorite papertag
Therefore G4's at the Clearport
When it come to tools fool I'm a Pep Boy
When it came to dope I was quick to export
Never tired of ballin' so it's on to the next sport
New Mercedes sedan, the Lex Sport
So many cars DMV thought it was mail fraud
Different traps I was getting mail from
Polk County, Jacksonville rep Melbourne
Whole clique's appetite had tapeworms
Spinning Teddy Pendergrass vinyl as my J burns
I shed a tear before the night's over
God bless the man I put this ice over
Getting 2Pac money twice over
Still a real nigga, red Coogi sweater, dice roller
I'm making love to the angel of death
Catching feelings, never stumble, retracing my steps

—"Devil in a New Dress,"
My Beautiful Dark Twisted Fantasy (2010)

When I got back from Hawaii I got started on *Teflon Don*. Working alongside the likes of Kanye and his mentor No I.D. inspired me to step up my production value. I made sure to get beats from both of them—Ye let me keep "Live Fast, Die Young" and No I.D. gifted me with "Tears of Joy." Then DJ Clark Kent of the legendary Supermen DJs came out of his semiretirement to bless me with *Teflon Don*'s first single, "Super High." Meanwhile J.U.S.T.I.C.E. League were busy cooking up the third chapter of "Maybach Music." If they were going to outdo all the arrangements and live instrumentation that they'd done on the second installment it was going to take a while.

I had all these elite producers getting involved in *Teflon Don* so it was funny when two beats from an unknown teenager set off the album. I think Lex Luger made "MC Hammer" and "B.M.F." in ten minutes.

I was at Central Station in Atlanta on the set of the "O Let's Do It" music video. "O Let's Do It" was the breakout release of Gucci Mane's protégé Waka Flocka Flame. In his mentor's absence—Gucci had gotten locked up again—Waka had picked up the 1017 Brick Squad torch and ran with it. He'd gotten Puff, Fabolous and myself to get on the remix to "O Let's Do It."

Waka had another record that was booming on the set that day. "Hard in da Paint." It was not a typical radio-friendly single. There was nothing friendly about it. It was sinister sounding and the way Waka was barking all over it made it even more menacing. I knew I could make something tough over a beat like that.

I had Spiff find out who the producer behind "Hard in da Paint" was so I could record my own version. It turned out to be an eighteen-year-old kid from Virginia going by the name Lex Luger. Waka had discovered him on Myspace and brought him down to Atlanta, where he'd spent six months in Waka's basement knocking out beats assembly line style on a TR–808 drum machine.

Lex sent over more than fifty beats, which Spiff filtered down to twenty or so he thought I might like. All of Lex's beats sounded similar, but he most definitely had his own sound. It was this batch of beats that led to "MC Hammer" and "B.M.F."

I was riding through the Hollywood Hills when I came up with "MC Hammer." I'd gone to Los Angeles to shoot the music video for "Super High." Afterward, as I was leaving the set to go back to my hotel, Stiff started running through Lex's beats. I was so high during that drive. I was smoking Cali's finest—my favorite strain, P.R. 80—and as I stared out the window and looked at all the mansions and sports cars all I kept thinking about was how MC Hammer was living in the nineties.

> My gun dirty, my brick clean
> I'm ridin' dirty, my dick clean
> She talk dirty, but her mouth clean
> Bitch, I'm MC Hammer, I'm about cream
> I got thirty cars, whole lot of dancers
> I take 'em everywhere, I'm MC Hammer
> Started sellin' dope, I'm too legit to quit
> When it's Hammer Time, I'm pullin' out the stick

—"MC Hammer,"
Teflon Don (2010)

I was super tight with Puff at this time. It got reported that Puff had come on board as my manager but there was never a formal arrangement like that. Basically Puff and I were partying together a lot then and a bunch of great music and business deals—I became an ambassador for his Cîroc vodka—got made in the process.

I flew up to New York to meet with Puff and explain to him my game plan. *Teflon Don* wasn't scheduled to come out for a couple months but I wanted to touch the streets now. I had a feeling Lex Luger was going to become the most in-demand producer in the industry and I wanted to be at the forefront of that sound. So I wanted to drop *The Albert Anastasia EP*, a prequel to *Teflon Don* and a sign of things to come.

Puff went crazy when I played "MC Hammer" for him at Daddy's House Studios in Midtown Manhattan. He was damn near begging me to let him get a verse on there. But he hated that I was planning on putting it on *Albert Anastasia*. He was dead set against it. This song was a fucking hit. I couldn't just drop it for free on Datpiff and LiveMixtapes. It would get lost in the sea of free music that was hitting the internet every day.

Over the course of my career Puff Daddy has been as important of an adviser to me as Tony Draper or Jay-Z or any other legend who I've been blessed to pick up game from. But just because someone is a great adviser doesn't mean you need to take every piece of their advice. I knew that it was time for me to feed the streets. *Deeper than Rap* had been critically acclaimed and earned me a lot of new fans. I was finally getting my respect as a lyricist. But I hadn't had an anthem like "Hustlin'" or "The Boss" in a while. Songs like "Maybach Music 2" were these intricate pieces of art but they weren't killing the clubs. "MC Hammer" was going to change that and I was going to drop it on the eve of Memorial Day weekend. I was going to set the tone for the whole summer.

On the morning of *The Albert Anastasia EP*'s release I recorded a song for the mixtape at the last minute—"B.M.F." "B.M.F." was another Lex Luger beat that Spiff had played for me one night in Washington, DC, when we were chilling on Khaled's tour bus. I zoned out to it for a while and eventually started mumbling a hook, which Spiff would transcribe on his Blackberry for us to revisit whenever we got back into the studio. Once Spiff got an iPhone we started recording voice memos but that was our creative process at the time.

I didn't get back to the beat until the night before its release when I finally wrote my verses to it. But I didn't even lay them down that night. I'd been hitting the road hard and my vocal cords were roasted again. I tried drinking some lemon honey tea and giving it a go but it wasn't working.

The next morning I decided to give it one last shot. E-Mix, my engineer, had to start mixing and mastering *Albert Anastasia* if we were going to put it out that night. My marketing and promotions ace, Lex Promo, needed to get the final track list so he could start printing CDs and hit the streets. And I had to leave to get on a flight somewhere. There was no more time left. I stepped into the booth and pushed "B.M.F." out in one take.

The crazy shit about "B.M.F." is how Styles P ended up on there. I had been talking about doing a record with Styles but not over one of Lex Luger's beats. I'd been thinking we'd do some East Coast, Yonkers, L.O.X. type shit. Not Atlanta trap. Styles's verse on the song is so hard I wish I could take credit for seeing the vision. But the truth is it was a total accident.

What happened was, when Lex Luger sent Spiff this batch of beats they were all numbered. He didn't name each one individually. After Spiff did his A&R duties and picked out the ones he thought I might like, he started circulating the rest to the other artists he was working with at the time. Styles was one of those artists. When Styles P sent Spiff back a verse on the "B.M.F." beat, Spiff realized his mistake. He'd accidentally sent him one of the beats meant for me.

"All of these got the same 808s," Spiff said. "I could just find another one to put his vocals on."

"Nah, but he killed that," I said. "Let's keep him on there."

That's how the "B.M.F." beat landed back on my radar right before the release of *Albert Anastasia*. We'd kind of forgotten about it until Styles sent Spiff his verse. That reminded me of how hard it was and how I'd come up with this hook for it that would have all the dope boys in an uproar.

I think I'm Big Meech, Larry Hoover
Whippin' work, Hallelujah
One nation, under God
Real niggas gettin' money from the fuckin' start

—"B.M.F. (Blowin' Money Fast),"
Teflon Don (2010)

The way the streets responded to "B.M.F." on Memorial Day weekend of 2010 was the closest thing to how it felt when I first dropped "Hustlin'."

I don't even think the song charted that high on the Billboard charts but it didn't have to. It was an anthem for the streets.

The anticipation for *Teflon Don* was through the roof and pretty soon I was ready to drop it. But it was still missing one thing. Once again, I was waiting on Jay-Z's vocals.

I'd gotten Jay-Z to appear on the second track of *Teflon Don* on a song called "Free Mason." But when Khaled went up to New York to finish mixing the album, he couldn't get the files from Jay's session. Guru, Jay-Z's engineer, told Khaled the hard drive the session was on had broken.

Khaled started to panic. He didn't really have a direct friendship with Jay-Z at the time, but he started blowing up his phone. Jay-Z didn't immediately respond so Khaled started texting every single person in his phone that knew Jay-Z. I wasn't there for any of this but the way Khaled tells the story he was lying down in the middle of Times Square texting Jay-Z's phone over and over again begging him to re-lay his verse. Khaled is so crazy.

But Hov always keeps it one hundred and comes through. He finally texted Khaled back that he was on vacation in the

Hamptons and that he would redo the verse as soon as he got back to the city. But *Teflon Don* had to get turned in the next day if we wanted to drop it on July 20, and it had already gotten pushed back twice. So Jay-Z had his engineer come to his crib in the Hamptons and bring all the studio equipment so he could finish the song for me before the deadline.

Khaled was still out of breath from the whole ordeal when he called me to tell me what happened. Khaled knows me well and he knew better than to bring me this problem until it was solved. I don't like to hear about that type of shit when I'm in album mode.

"My nerves are so bad right now," he told me. "But I got it done, Rozay. I got it done."

"I know you don't think I believe that story, Khaled," I told him. "Who the fuck drops Jay-Z's hard drive on the train?"

"You don't believe me?" Khaled said. "You can ask Guru!"

"If anything, Jay probably heard me body my verse on there and it made him want to redo his," I told him.

I didn't actually think that. I was just fucking with Khaled. I told him he should probably go see a doctor because he seemed stressed. He told me that he'd already seen several.

With "Free Mason" complete, my fourth album was ready to go. When it came out a few weeks later the response was unanimous. *Teflon Don* was my magnum opus.

Teflon Don *is Rick Ross' fourth solo album, and the one that establishes him as one of rap's most potent and creative forces. He's a ferocious character, an impressive rapper and, as heard on this strong album, a clever and loose thinker, willing to try out new poses.*
    —The New York Times

At just 11 songs, Teflon Don *is Ross's slimmest and also strongest album. His goals remain the same: acquire wealth, explain wealth.*

*But his word choice and onomatopoetic gestures are unmatched in
rap right now. It is by turns lush, pummeling and delirious, rip-
pling with an '80s cheese that translates stunningly well to rap.*

—The Washington Post

*Ross has proven to be among the last of a dying breed. His stu-
dio albums feel like events that demand the ears and opinions of
rap fans.*

—Pitchfork

CHAPTER
15

THE LOVE *TEFLON DON* WAS GETTING FROM
the critics was most definitely appreciated. But no album review
can compare to the feeling of having someone tell you your
music got them through some shit. That is the ultimate com-
pliment. Especially when that someone is Lil Wayne.

Wayne called me from Rikers Island right after the album
came out. He was halfway through a one-year bid he'd received
after getting caught with a pistol in New York City. He'd heard
"I'm Not a Star"—the album's intro—on Hot 97 and he told
me the song spoke to him. He wanted to make a song just like
that when he got out. I had a record ready for him when he did.
That song became known as "John."

The other thing I took away from that phone call was that
Wayne wasn't being supported by his people the way he deserved to be in his time of need. Considering how many records Wayne had sold for Cash Money Records over the last

decade I thought that was shameful. After the release of *Teflon Don* I'd turned my attention to building out my label and that conversation was one of the things that got me thinking about the kind of executive I wanted to be.

The first artist I wanted to sign to Maybach Music Group was Wiz Khalifa. Spiff had put me onto Wiz and I'd gotten him and Curren$y to hop on the remix to "Super High." I got the opportunity to meet Wiz properly after I flew him and Curren$y to Atlanta to shoot a video for the song.

Not only was Wiz making dope music but he was savvier than his stoner persona let on. Wiz was ahead of the curve when it came to using the internet and social media to build a fan base and he had a grassroots movement behind him. His *Kush & OJ* mixtape had been a worldwide trending topic on Twitter for days following its release. For a mixtape with no major label dollars behind it, that was quite an accomplishment. Meanwhile I'd just found out what Twitter was a few months earlier when I was in Hawaii.

I knew that Wiz was a superstar in the making. So I was disappointed when I didn't have the resources at my disposal to do a deal with him. I didn't have deep enough pockets to compete with the likes of Atlantic Records, where he ended up signing. That was frustrating, especially after I'd announced my intention to sign him during an episode of MTV's *RapFix*. I tried to speak it into existence and it didn't work. But I didn't allow that disappointment to discourage me. I used it as motivation.

I still owed a few solo albums to Def Jam but I wanted to find a different home for MMG. Things hadn't been the same there since Shakir passed. I'd gotten a taste of having my own imprint but Maybach's one release—the group album with Triple C's, *Custom Cars & Cycles*—didn't do numbers, and the other artists I'd tried bringing to the label hadn't gotten much support from the staff.

Once again I was the subject of a bidding war. Jimmy Iovine and Puff wanted me to bring Maybach to Interscope and Bad Boy. There was interest from Roc Nation. Khaled had just signed to Cash Money and he and Birdman were trying to get me to come there.

In the end it was Warner Bros. Records that won the MMG sweepstakes. At the top of 2011 I got a call from Dallas Martin. Dallas had been an intern under Shakir when I first signed to Def Jam in 2006. I used to see him at Hitco Studios in Atlanta while I was working on *Port of Miami* and *Trilla*. Shakir would have him in there listening to demos from sunup to sundown. Dallas never had a hand in my music then but I could see his drive.

Dallas ended up getting let go after Shakir passed so I was happy to see he'd landed back on his feet. Joie Manda, the head of urban music at Warner Bros., had hired him as vice president of A&R. Joie and Dallas wanted to pitch me on the idea of bringing MMG to Warner Bros so I had them meet me in Toronto where I had a show that upcoming weekend. That was the weekend Drake lent me his Maybach so Spiff and I could shoot a visual for "Devil in a New Dress."

Dallas had an ear that was trained and fine-tuned by Shakir Stewart, the sharpest A&R I'd ever worked with. He knew the ingredients of a hit record and he was someone I could trust to work with any artists that I signed on a day-to-day basis. Then there was Joie. Joie had a strong track record from his days at Asylum, where he'd facilitated a joint venture with Swishahouse, the Houston label behind the rise of Mike Jones, Paul Wall and Chamillionaire. That alliance had paved the way for the Houston Rap takeover of the mid-2000s. And I was told I'd have the full support of the two top dogs at Warner, Lyor Cohen and Todd Moscowitz, who wanted to co-manage me alongside Pucci.

We finalized the deal during NBA All-Star Weekend in Los Angeles. Right away I announced my first two signings. I'd been scouting for talent since the summer.

I first met Wale at King of Diamonds. From the little I knew of him at the time, Wale was a backpack rapper. A pure lyricist and uncut emcee. So I was surprised to see him in a strip club, and I was even more surprised to hear his music booming in there. He had a record with Waka Flocka Flame and Roscoe Dash called "No Hands" that was burning the place down.

"No Hands" was a hit record but it wasn't an accurate representation of Wale as an artist. Wale had depth. He could make a strip club anthem but he also made songs that resonated with women on a deeper level. He was the poster boy of the blogs but he also had the HBCUs and his hometown of Washington, DC, behind him. His music paid tribute to his Nigerian heritage and had elements of Go-Go and spoken word poetry.

But Wale's talents hadn't been fully tapped into. His buzz on the blogs had gotten him a deal at Interscope but he'd since been dropped from the label. His debut album, *Attention Deficit*, had flopped. But I wasn't concerned about the numbers he'd put up or what the conversation surrounding his career was. Wale got my attention by how talented he was. I told him I was in the process of figuring out MMG's label situation and if he could hang tight I wanted to bring him on board.

A few months later I was in Philadelphia for a press run ahead of the release of *Teflon Don*. When I got there I surveyed my new Twitter followers—since my trip to Hawaii I'd figured it out—to see which artists from the city my fans wanted to see me work with. The overwhelming response was Meek Mill. I had a radio interview at Power 99 the next day and DJ Cosmic Kev invited Meek to the station so we could meet.

Meek showed up to the station wearing a black Burberry polo

and a backpack. He was a tall, skinny kid with nappy cornrows and I gathered that designer polo was the nicest shirt he owned. He was getting every last possible fit out of it—you know how polo collars curl up when they start to wear out?

Meek was twenty-three but had been battle rapping on Philly corners since he was fourteen. His *Flamers* mixtapes had gotten the attention of T.I., who signed him to Grand Hustle in 2008. But due to their legal troubles—Meek had to serve six months on gun and drug charges and T.I. caught his own federal case— the deal never went anywhere. So Meek was a free agent.

Meek had a song called "Rosé Red" that was buzzing and he asked me if I would hop on the remix. I was charging close to six figures for a verse at the time but I told him I'd do it off the strength. I had a feeling about Meek. He had the grit and fero- ciousness of the great rappers who came from the city of broth- erly love before him—niggas like Beanie Sigel and Freeway—but his music was more than punchlines and double entendres. Meek had heart. He reminded me of Tupac. The kid was going places. Before we parted ways, Meek asked if there was someone in my camp he could stay in contact with. I gave him my personal number and we were in touch from that point on.

Months later, as I was getting close to finalizing my deal with Warner Bros., I had my sister fly Meek down to Miami so that we could talk about his future. The next morning, right after I got word that Meek had landed and was on his way to the house, Renee called. She sounded flustered.

"Will, I'm sorry, I messed up," she said. "I booked Meek's flight under your name and I accidentally did it backward. I must be losing my mind."

"He's on his way over to the house though."

That's when we realized Meek's government name was Rob- ert Williams. I took that as a sign. This was a partnership that was meant to be. When Meek got to my house I showed him

$10 million in cash in a duffel bag and I told him this is what we would start working toward if he signed with MMG. He took that as a sign as well. We inked the paperwork that day.

Then there was Pill, a rapper out of Atlanta. Warner Bros. had signed Pill a year before after he got himself a buzz off a song called "Trap Goin' Ham." He'd gotten cosigned by Andre 3000 and earned a spot on *XXL* magazine's Freshman List, but there seemed to be little progress on rolling out a debut album. The label didn't really know what to do with him so I agreed to bring him into the fold and see what progress he could make under the MMG umbrella.

I thought it would take a minute to get MMG off the ground and up and running. But everybody came out the gates swinging. Meek immediately established himself as one of the most talked about prospects in the game with a one-two punch of singles, "Tupac Back" and "Ima Boss." Wale was proving himself worthy of a second chance at stardom. His showcase effort on *Self Made*, a song called "That Way" that featured Jeremih and myself, took off as he started building momentum toward his upcoming solo album, *Ambition*.

The success we were seeing energized me. I signed two new artists that spring, an emcee from Ohio named Stalley and a singer named Teedra Moses. I wasn't done. I signed a young brother from Chicago named Rockie Fresh. I wanted a West Coast artist so I tried to sign Nipsey Hussle and Dom Kennedy. I wanted to plant the MMG flag in New York so I tried to sign French Montana. Those ones didn't end up working out for different reasons but I built relationships with all of them and tried to help them however I could regardless. Puff had put a deal on the table for French I couldn't match but French wanted me to executive produce his debut album anyway. MMG was something artists wanted to be involved with even if we never made it official on paper. I loved that.

My momentum was cut short that fall when I boarded a Delta flight in Fort Lauderdale. I was headed to Memphis where I was scheduled to perform at the University of Memphis's "Midnight Madness" event. I was with my on-and-off girlfriend Shateria, Pucci, Sam Sneak, and Toie and Will.

I went to sleep as soon as I got to my seat. I'd been going hard and my schedule wasn't slowing down anytime soon. At least I had this two-hour flight to catch up on some rest.

When I opened my eyes my whole team was surrounding me. Shateria was crying and everybody else looked pretty shaken up too.

"They're turning the plane around," Pucci said. "They saying you just had a seizure?"

I had no recollection of whatever had just happened. My shoulder was hurting but otherwise I felt fine. I saw no reason for me to miss my show that night. But the flight crew wasn't hearing it. They wanted me off the plane.

"Okay, well, we still getting to the bag later," I told Pucci. "I just did the Electric Slide!"

Nobody found my joke as funny as I did. It turns out having a seizure is scarier for the people there to witness it than it is for the person having one.

As soon as we deplaned I had my sister hit up my jet plug and arrange for a private flight to take us to Memphis. An hour later we were back in the air. Fifteen minutes in I had another seizure.

When I opened my eyes after the second seizure I was in a dreamlike state. It wasn't like when I'd woken up from the first one and everything was fine. I felt groggy and my vision was blurry. I didn't know where I was or how I'd gotten there. I definitely wasn't on a jet. Then I saw a gun. I figured I must be in the afterlife.

Damn…somebody got me.

As my vision slowly came back into focus I saw that the gun I'd seen was holstered on the hip of a police officer standing at my bedside. I was not in Heaven. I was in the hospital.

"Where am I?"

"This is UAB Hospital in Birmingham, Alabama," he said. "I got your back, Boss."

I wasn't waking up from a seizure. I had just woken up from surgery and my hazy hallucination was a result of anesthesia. In the course of my first seizure I'd dislocated my shoulder and I had a torn labrum. I remember my shoulder felt all fucked up when I boarded the private jet. After the orthopedic surgeon explained the details of my shoulder surgery, a neurologist came into the room.

The doctors attached electrodes to my head and performed an EEG test. There were no abnormalities in my brain activity that would indicate I had epilepsy. They did an MRI and CT scan and the results were the same. At first the neurologist didn't have a diagnosis for me but after I told him a little about my lifestyle he had a few theories.

The doctor was concerned about the lack of sleep I was getting. I rarely slept for more than a couple of hours at a time. I could blame that on my schedule but really it had more to do with my restlessness. Even if I got into bed at a reasonable hour I would always just lie there awake for hours. My thoughts would start to wander and they just wouldn't stop wandering. It had been like that for years.

My diet and different vices weren't helping either. I didn't have the healthiest habits. The doctor was alarmed by the amount of weed I smoked but he didn't think that had caused the seizures. He did think the Tuss may have played a part.

I first started drinking Tussionex a few years back, in the midst of the correctional officer controversy and my war with 50 Cent. In hindsight I think I picked up the habit to cope with the stress I was under at the time.

Tussionex is prescription cough syrup. It's prescribed to people with chronic bronchitis and emphysema. Its primary ingredient is hydrocodone, and hydrocodone is like codeine. They're both opioids. They slow down your central nervous system. But hydrocodone does so in a more powerful way. See, a lot of rappers drink codeine and promethazine cough syrup, myself included at the time, but not a lot of rappers drink Tuss. The lean is purple. You mix it with Sprite. The Tuss is yellow. You drink it straight. It's too strong to drink socially so it was not some cool rapper shit. I never broadcast my usage for the cameras. It was something I did mostly by myself.

"I'm going to prescribe you some anti-seizure medication but you need to start taking better care of yourself," the doctor said. "Get more sleep and cut it out with that stuff you're putting in your body."

I am a person motivated by opposition. So much of my success has been fueled by having an opponent across from me. Sometimes these enemies are real, as was the case with 50 Cent. Sometimes they are figments of my imagination, like when I was convinced Ted Lucas and DJ Khaled were holding me back. Either way that war-mode mentality brings out the best in me. It is the thing that pushes me to keep going when I have all the reasons in the world to give up. But this time the enemy was myself. My body and my brain had betrayed me. I didn't know how to make sense of that.

At that moment my momma busted into the room and gave me the biggest hug of my life. She started to cry and then she started to pray. I don't live with a lot of fear but as I held on to my momma that day I'd never been so afraid.

I went unconscious I woke up to see my momma smile
She told me no more promethazine, that'll make her proud
Think about it, damn I had to think about it
Give me a second momma, let me think about it

—"Smile Mama, Smile,"
Black Market (2015)

Khaled came to the hospital to get me. I didn't even ask him to. As soon as he heard what happened he was blowing up Renee's and Pucci's phones trying to find out where I was. He came as soon as he found out.

Khaled is deathly afraid of flying. I believe he may have since conquered that fear but I know that when this happened he still hadn't because he'd just spent $500,000 on a new tour bus. When he showed up to the hospital he told me it was at my full disposal. I think Khaled was more worried about me flying than I was.

"Rozay, I'm telling you, I'll take you wherever you want," he said. "But please, do not get back on one of those airplanes."

Khaled drove me to my momma's house in Memphis, where I spent the next two weeks on bedrest. It was the most time I'd taken off since before "Hustlin'." I spent the time reading Scripture, enjoying my kids' company and my momma's cooking. Khaled and his wife, Nicole, stayed with me the whole time. Khaled was still working at 99 Jamz but he recorded all of his radio spots on the tour bus's mini-studio so he could stay with me. That's the kind of friend DJ Khaled is.

After taking some time off to recover from surgery and the seizures I was ready to get back to my music. I had an album's worth of material ready to go. But before I could put anything out, I needed to have a sit-down with Def Jam.

My relationship with the label had gradually deteriorated after L.A. Reid left to become chairman and CEO of Epic Records.

He'd been the last of the original trio that signed me in '06. I wasn't really tripping over L.A., Jay and Shakir not being there though. I no longer needed the same kind of hands-on guidance I'd gotten when I was just getting started. I had my own team in-house now. What I needed from Def Jam was money. I'd outgrown the terms of my original contract and we needed to restructure my deal to account for that.

Khaled was my last remaining point of contact at the label. Always a peacekeeper, he convinced Barry Weiss, Def Jam's new CEO, and his staff to fly down to Miami so we could try to come to an agreement. He set up a lunch meeting at Prime One Twelve. I made it a point to show up an hour late and then immediately proceeded to cuss out everybody there. These people were not treating me like a top priority and they needed to understand the severity of that mistake.

Khaled started kicking me under the table. Beads of sweat gathered on his forehead.

"Ross, can you please chill the fuck out!" he whispered.

"Oh and by the way… I don't like how y'all have been treating Khaled either!"

Then I stood up and walked out, leaving Khaled to clean up the mess I'd just made.

"You've got a real funny way of showing love, you know that?" he told me later.

If the label wanted to play hardball I was just going to drop this music as a mixtape and go tour off it. That would only give me more leverage when I sat back down at the bargaining table with Def Jam.

The label dispute was the reason behind the release of *Rich Forever*, a mixtape originally intended to be my fifth album. Everybody was telling me I couldn't just drop these records with Nas, Drake and John Legend for free. It was the same story Puff had given me about "MC Hammer" and "B.M.F."

I knew I might lose out on some short-term record sales but in the long run this was only going to boost my stock. My motto has always been if it ain't a long-term play then it's just small talk. When I dropped *Rich Forever* at the top of 2012 my bet on myself proved to be a smart one. The format of the release didn't matter. The music spoke for itself.

Rich Forever meets a standard of quality control that's rare for albums, let alone mixtapes: 18 new songs, all of them good, many of them exhilarating—chief among them the exultant 'Keys To The Crib,' and 'Triple Beam Dreams,' a courtroom drama featuring an elaborate Nas verse that's downright Illmatic-*worthy. It's a big project, but it never drags, overreaches, or stumbles; Ross rhymes throughout with so much power and economy that it just keeps barreling forward. If he can sustain this remarkable stride, Ross could probably pull off a double album if he wanted to.*
—*The A.V. Club*

With clusters of meaty verses and throbbing, moody production, Rich Forever *is almost on par with his last two solo albums,* Deeper Than Rap *and* Teflon Don, *both great. In just a few years he's become a real bear of a rapper. Powerful, indignant, protective: that's how a bear feels, and that's how Mr. Ross sounds, as if nothing could possibly derail him, and everyone who walks with him will be safe.*
—*The New York Times*

Rick Ross' new mixtape, possibly his best full-length, finds the Teflon Don moving out of his comfort zone and entering a world where it feels like something is at stake.
—*Pitchfork*

Rich Forever was a showcase of my second signature sound. My first was what I call the Maybach sound. Luxurious, soulful songs like "Maybach Music" and "Cigar Music" that transport listeners into another tax bracket. *Rich Forever* was all street records. It was the sound I'd tapped into with Lex Luger on songs like "B.M.F." and "MC Hammer" and continued to refine on *Self Made Vol. 1. Rich Forever* was me perfecting it.

Then I went on a fourteen-date European tour and made all the money that I'd asked Def Jam for myself. At that point the label decided to give in to my demands. They realized the longer they let this situation play out, the more it was going to end up costing them. Once Def Jam cut the check I got to work on *God Forgives, I Don't.*

I'd gone big with every one of my albums but this one was going to be the biggest. I wanted this album to play out like a blockbuster film. I'd been inspired by the works of Mario Puzzo, Quentin Tarantino and Martin Scorsese. I wanted the track list for *God Forgives, I Don't* to look like Scorsese's cast for *The Departed*, when he somehow managed to cast Jack Nicholson, Leo DiCaprio, Matt Damon, Mark Wahlberg and Alec Baldwin all in one movie. This would be something epic like that.

From day one of me making music Dr. Dre had been my idol. As a youngster my record collection was filled with Ruthless Records albums and the idea of one day getting in the studio with Dre had been a lifelong dream. When I was in Hawaii working with Kanye on *My Beautiful Dark Twisted Fantasy*, those studio sessions were what I imagined it must have been like when Dre made *The Chronic.* This genius piecing together a masterpiece made up from all these different contributions.

But out of respect for Dre I never pursued us working together. I knew it might put him in uncomfortable position, with 50 Cent being signed to Aftermath. The last thing I wanted was to cause problems for one of my biggest influences so I let that dream lie. But I didn't let it die.

I ended up connecting with The D.O.C., who cowrote *The*

Chronic with Dre, and we got to chopping it up about Dre's place in hip-hop's pantheon. To my surprise, D.O.C. told me that the respect was mutual. A few days later he got me on the phone with Dre, who said he was going to be in Miami in a few weeks and we should lock in. Of course I cleared my schedule.

Dre came to Miami bearing gifts. Dre had gotten this beat from an A&R at Aftermath. It was produced by Jake One and sampled a gospel record called "I'm So Grateful" by Crowns of Glory. It reminded me of a record I'd done recently with Drake called "Lord Knows." I wrote verses for both us and we knocked the song out that first day at Circle House Studios. We didn't finish it though. There was one thing left to do to make this collaboration bigger than it already was. Of course I had to get Jay-Z on there. I'd already made plans to get Jay-Z on a different song for *God Forgives, I Don't*, but that one could wait. He needed to be on this. And that's how "3 Kings" was born.

If I was getting Dre and Hov on records together I figured I might as well shoot my shot and see what other collaborations I could cross off my bucket list. I'd gotten this beat from J.U.S.T.I.C.E League that sounded like vintage Outkast. Through the powers that be I was able to get on a Skype call with the elusive Andre 3000, who was somewhere in Europe filming a Jimi Hendrix biopic.

I told Andre how fourteen years earlier I'd opened for Outkast at Studio 183 in Carol City. I wasn't even Teflon da Don then. I was still rapping as Willow. Outkast was in town for a prerecord release party ahead of their third album, *Aquemini*. A week before the show the promoter hosted a competition where you could come up to Studio 183 and present a song. Whoever had the best one got to open for Outkast. It ended up being me.

Opening for Outkast is going to be memorable on any day, but this one was special for another reason. It was Friday, September 11, 1998. It was the day the feds arrested Jabbar. That

was the reason I wasn't up there in Jacksonville. I'd gone back
to Miami to open for Outkast.

This was the first time Andre 3000 and I ever spoke so I wasn't
going to get into that whole story. I just told him I'd opened up
for him and Big Boi back in the day and what an honor it was
for us to be talking about making some music. Andre loved the
beat and was all for getting on there but being the innovator he
is, doing a "vintage Outkast" record wasn't enough. We got to
talking about going outside the box, breaking the mold of hip-
hop's standard sixteen-bar verse. Sixteen wasn't enough either.
This talk culminated in the eight-minute long epic "Sixteen"
where Andre delivered me a classic verse and an electric guitar
solo at the end. 3 Stacks went full Jimi on that bitch.

Then I got some more features from Drake, Usher and Ne-Yo.
I got beats from Pharrell. These things don't come cheap so I used
every bit of my recording budget from Def Jam and then I asked
for some more. The uncredited feature from L.A. Reid on "Maybach Music IV" didn't cost me a dime though. Some things in life
are priceless. That was a little wink at the label, just like the one
I'd given Atlantic Records on "Hustlin'" back in '05.

With all these layered components, God Forgives *is a deep record
that trips listeners on each listen… With its share of both musical indulgence and serious self-reflection, it's an album as big and
sturdy as the man behind it.*

                                                    —Consequence of Sound

*It's a thrillingly specific set of images, delivered in Ross' signature
cocksure wheeze—and helps make the big-check brags all the more
endearing. Sure, he's been bragging about his rep since his 2006
debut, but* God Forgives *is the first album that really feels like
it was made by a boss.*

                                                    —Entertainment Weekly

There are self-aware moments here too that feel new for a Rick Ross record... On this commanding, complicated album, he wants more out of more.

—*The Los Angeles Times*

God Forgives, I Don't did the biggest numbers of my career. For the fourth time my album had debuted at number one on the Billboard charts and for the first time I'd broken the 200,000 benchmark with first-week sales of 218,000 copies. A month later it was certified Gold. I felt like Scorsese winning Best Picture at the Academy Awards.

CHAPTER

16

MY THIRTY-SIXTH YEAR HAD BEEN FILLED with blessings. It was only right I ring in my thirty-seventh in style. We did it real big that night. As a matter of fact, we did it big that whole weekend. After taking over Club Compound in Atlanta on Saturday I flew back to the crib Sunday for my birthday party at LIV. I had on an all-white suit with a red button-up underneath and velvet Versace Medusa slippers on my feet. And I had a big-ass gold Cuban link around my neck. I looked like Tony Montana when he went to meet Sosa in Cochabamba. I didn't know I'd be living like Scarface in more ways than one that night.

We turned LIV into The Babylon. Everybody was in the club that night. Puff was there. French was there. Fabolous. Ludacris. Christina Milian. Scott Storch. The whole MMG family was there. All of my day one Carol City niggas were there. Shateria was by my side in a black minidress and thigh-high boots.

We were popping bottles of Luc Belaire. We were smoking big blunts. We were eating birthday cake. It was just one of those nights.

I left the club a little after 4:00 a.m. I got into a silver Rolls-Royce Phantom with Shateria. Black and one of my security guards were behind me in the van. As I crossed the bridge that connects Miami Beach to the Miami I knew, I had a moment of introspection. Where I came from a lot of niggas never make it to the beach. But I had. And I'd made it a lot further than the Fontainebleau.

I hopped on I-95 and headed home. As I approached the exit toward Fort Lauderdale I called Black and told him I could take it from there. I was going to my house in Seven Isles. Everybody else was staying at the studio house in Davie. They didn't need to drive the extra hour at five in the morning so they could escort me the rest of the way home. At least I thought they didn't.

Five minutes from the house I stopped at a red light on the corner of Las Olas Boulevard and 15th Avenue. Shateria and I were in the middle of an argument over a chick she'd seen me talking to in the club when I heard the shots.

Pop! Pop! Pop! Pop! Pop! Pop! Pop! Pop!

"911, what is your emergency?"

"I just heard a bunch of gunshots go off and a car sped by. And my server just left on her bike to go to a— Oh my God they're turning around and coming back! I'm hanging up! I'm hanging up! Bye!"

"Okay, ma'am, how many shots did you hear?"

"I don't know! I don't know! But they're coming back! I'm hiding!"

Witnesses would later tell police they saw four men pull up in a maroon BMW and open fire. But I didn't see the shooters. I didn't see the car either. I only heard the shots. From the sound of them I could tell they came from sticks. They were too loud and too fast to have come from a handgun.

I hit the gas and peeled off. I turned off Las Olas onto 15th Avenue but I overshot my turn. I was driving drunk, high and barefoot. My daddy always told me never to drive barefoot.

I had leaned to my right side and tried to cover Shateria but before I could look up and straighten out the wheel I lost control of my car and crashed into the apartment building behind The Floridian diner. The airbags exploded in our faces.

When I went to open my door I couldn't. It was jammed. I looked to Shateria.

"Run!"

Shateria got out on the passenger side and took off running behind the building. I finally managed to open my door and went out to follow her. Then I heard the screeching sound of a car turning around on Las Olas. They were coming back around.

Please tell me Shateria did not just run behind the house we crashed into. That's the first place they're gonna check. Any house but that one.

I ran back to the car and grabbed my Cuban link. These niggas weren't getting away with my chain. That piece was four kilos of solid gold. It had cost me $160,000. Then I grabbed my chrome Smith & Wesson 9mm that had fallen between the seats in the crash. I wasn't going to leave Shateria but I wasn't going to be caught empty-handed when these shooters found us.

I ran behind the building but I couldn't find Shateria. It was five in the morning so I couldn't see anything. The backyard was fenced in so I knew she had to be here somewhere. There was only one way in and one way out. I pulled my pistol from my waistband and prepared for a standoff. A full clip held fifteen rounds but I didn't know how many were loaded at that moment. Hopefully enough to get us out of there.

By the grace of God I wouldn't need any bullets. After the shooters pulled the U-turn on Las Olas they took off north up 16th Avenue.

I finally found Shateria curled up in a ball hiding under the back porch. She was shaking so hard at first I thought she'd been hit. She hadn't but she was damn near having a panic attack. Shateria was hyperventilating when I found her. She'd heard my footsteps when I came back there but couldn't see if it was me from underneath the porch. So she just stayed there silently.

The police arrived a couple minutes later and taped off the crime scene. Eighteen bullet casings were found scattered through the streets and two storefronts. But they hadn't hit the car. Were they actually trying to kill me and missed badly or were they just trying to send a message?

The detectives took Shateria and I inside the diner to take down our statements. They started asking a whole bunch of police-ass questions.

"Do you have any idea who did this?"

"I don't."

"Well, we know who you are... Do you think this may have had something to do with the Carol City Cartel?"

"Triple C's is a music group."

"Right... What about the Gangster's Disciples? Isn't it true you've been having problems with them?"

"Who?"

"Didn't you have to cancel some shows recently?"

"I have no idea what you're talking about."

"What about 50 Cent?"

"The donkey?"

"Excuse me?"

"Detectives, with all due respect, my lawyer can help you answer the rest of your questions. It's been a long night. I need to get some rest."

"Look, we're just trying to get to the bottom of what happened."

"Me too. Good luck with that."

Black Bo and Pucci had showed up by then and he wanted to

know what happened too. I told him to have my sister get rooms for everybody at the St. Regis. This had taken place so close to the house that I knew Shateria wouldn't be able to sleep there.

My fresh-off-the-lot Phantom was now sitting on the back of a flatbed tow truck. The whole front was caved in. So Shateria and I got a driver to come take us to Bal Harbour. The sun was up by then and I was exhausted. Staying up all night drinking and smoking was pretty standard for me but surviving a drive-by shooting was not. I'd escaped the situation running on adrenaline but now I was fading fast.

We'd be at the hotel soon. There we would get to the bottom of all this. My momma and Renee were on their way to Miami. My lawyer was too. We could all debrief at the hotel. In the meantime I needed to take a quick nap.

When I opened my eyes I saw a look of horror on Shateria's face. She was hysterical. Something had just happened. I looked out the window and saw we were still in Fort Lauderdale. I hadn't been asleep longer than five minutes. But I'd missed something.

"Take us to the hospital!" she cried out. "Please! He's having a seizure!"

From the outside looking in 2012 had been a year of total domination. I'd graced the cover of *The Source*'s "Man of the Year" issue for the second year in a row. Then I topped MTV's Hottest MCs list. *God Forgives, I Don't* was the biggest album of my career. Meek and Wale were both flourishing under MMG.

But the year had not gone as smoothly as it seemed. The drive-by shooting on my birthday was the culmination of everything that had been bubbling beneath the surface.

When I first put out "B.M.F.," a group of niggas claiming to be Gangster's Disciples felt some type of way about me mentioning Larry Hoover, the Chicago gang's incarcerated leader. I was clearly saluting Hoover in the song so their intentions seemed suspect from the jump but out of respect for the OG, I met with Larry Hoover Jr. while I was in Chicago promoting the release of *Teflon Don*. He assured me his old man didn't have any problems with me. And that was pretty much that.

The situation, which was never anything to begin with, was dead for two years until I put out a mixtape called *The Black Bar Mitzvah*. Now this group of so-called GDs were claiming I'd used the gang's six-pointed star without permission and were making threats. It was so obvious that it was a Star of David on the mixtape cover and not the GD symbol. At that point I knew what the situation was. This was an extortion attempt and unfortunately for these niggas no checks were getting cut.

The week of *The Black Bar Mitzvah*'s release I had an altercation with the other person who had had a problem with "B.M.F.," Young Jeezy. Jeezy had run with Big Meech and BMF in their heyday and for some reason he felt some type of way over me paying homage to his OG. Over the years Jeezy and I had done several records together—he'd been on the "Hustlin'" remix back in '06—but ever since "B.M.F." he'd been slick dissing and sending little subliminal shots my way. Of course I'd paid him back in kind.

So when I saw Jeezy backstage at the 2012 BET Hip-Hop Awards in Atlanta I approached him so we could sort out any issues that needed to get sorted out. To me this whole thing was petty so I was ready to squash any beef. But I was also ready for any smoke if Jeezy wanted to go that route. Unfortunately we didn't get to come to an understanding. Our crews collided and we were quickly separated by police.

Gunplay should not have even been at the BET Hip-Hop Awards in the first place. He was on the run for armed robbery and assault with a deadly weapon stemming from an incident that took place at his accountant's office earlier that year.

Gunplay wasn't there when the situation with Jeezy went down but he caught wind there had been a commotion. When he started bouncing around trying to find out what had happened nobody would give him a straight answer. Everybody knew better than to tell Gunplay something that was going to rile him up. People were trying to de-escalate this situation.

But Gunplay Murdoch is not a person who needs to know all the specifics of a situation before diving into it headfirst. He figured if MMG had just gotten into it with some niggas then it had to have been 50 and G-Unit. So when Gunplay saw 50 and his secret service security team in the parking lot he decided to knuckle up against all eight of them. A melee ensued and Gunplay lost his chain and then he got hit with the sting of a thousand bees. Security pepper sprayed him and he scrambled into 2 Chainz's trailer before he got someone to get him the fuck out of there.

Don't even ask why Gunplay was out there by himself. You've got to ask that crazy motherfucker why he rolls like that. That's just Gunplay.

I say all that to say I'd been having problems with a lot of niggas. So when the police asked me who shot up my Phantom I told them I had no clue who it could have been.

I am not in the business of opening up investigations nor will I ever participate in one. But I will say that wasn't the first time niggas tried to kill me that year. There had been another incident. One that never made the news. It was similar to what happened on my birthday. Same type of situation. The same sound of a chopper ringing off. Except I wasn't with Shateria in my Phantom. I was in a Maybach. It didn't go down by my house in Seven Isles. It happened someplace else. And we didn't crash the car that time. I hopped out and started blowing it. I've said too much. Let's leave it there.

My favorite portion of the Bible is Psalms 27 1:4. Having

seen the things that I've seen I've interpreted it as a picture of a young nigga surviving death. I've carried these verses with me during dark moments.

The Lord is my light and my salvation—whom shall I fear? The Lord is the stronghold of my life—of whom shall I be afraid?

When the wicked advance against me to devour me, it is my enemies and my foes who will stumble and fall.

Though an army besiege me, my heart will not fear; though war break out against me, even then I will be confident.

One thing I ask from the Lord, this only do I seek; that I may dwell in the house of the Lord all the days of my life, to gaze on the beauty of the Lord, and to seek him in his temple.

Like I was saying, I have no idea who tried to take my life. But if I had to bet? I'd bet that it had nothing to do with any of that lame industry bullshit you read about on the blogs. I'd bet that it was about something else. And I'd bet you every shooter in the hit squad is dead as a doornail.

CHAPTER

17

HOMES HAVE ALWAYS BEEN A SOURCE OF inspiration for me. Both of my parents had been involved in real estate and passed down the importance of ownership and equity to my sister and me. They didn't believe in putting their savings in the stock market. They wanted to be able to touch their money. My daddy used to tell me that you haven't done your job as a man until you can provide a home for your family.

Back when Jabbar and I used to traffic work to Atlanta I would always have him take me by the Holyfield estate before we headed home. 794 Evander Holyfield Highway in Fayetteville, Georgia. We'd pull over to the side of the road, smoke half a joint and just take it all in.

Lord have mercy.

Villa Vittoriosa. "The Victory." I'd first seen the property featured on an episode of ESPN's *Sportscenter*. The former heavyweight champ had just had it built, and it was a sight to behold. A 45,000-square-foot mansion on a sprawling 105 acres.

The place had everything. Twelve bedrooms. Twenty-one bathrooms. A dining room that could fit one hundred guests. A movie theater. A bowling alley. An indoor basketball court. A tennis court. A softball field. A seven-stall horse barn. Behind the house was the largest residential swimming pool in the United States. Of course it had an indoor pool as well.

In 2006, right after *Port of Miami* went Gold, I bought my first million-dollar crib a mile away from the estate. So I would always ride by and admire the Holyfield house just like I used to back in '96. Then one day, in the fall of 2013, I saw a For Sale sign on the gate. I immediately called the phone number on the listing.

Evander Holyfield's property had gone into foreclosure and was now owned by JPMorgan Chase & Company. It was another sad story in boxing's history of former greats gone broke. Joe Louis died penniless and addicted to drugs. Leon Spinks went from beating Muhammad Ali in the Las Vegas Hilton to cleaning toilets at a YMCA in Nebraska. Mike Tyson made $300 million over the course of his career and went bankrupt. And Holyfield couldn't keep up with his child support payments for his twelve kids and six baby mothers.

Everybody was warning me about the costs of maintaining a place like this. They said the upkeep cost more than a million dollars annually. Christmas lights alone ran up a $17,000 electric bill. But I had to have this house. It felt like my destiny.

I'd sell my home in Seven Isles if I that's what it took. I'd paid $5,000,000 for a three-story mansion with eight bedrooms, a movie theater, an arcade and a gym. It was right on the water and I had a ninety-foot yacht named *Rich Forever* floating out back. That place was incredible. But it wasn't the Holyfield house.

This home was a symbol of possibility. The place I used

to dream of when I had nothing could now be mine. And it wouldn't just be mine. This would be something that belonged to my entire family that they could enjoy and be proud of. Somewhere my kids could bring all their friends and cousins and have the time of their lives.

I was still on the fence about purchasing the property until I had the opportunity to meet the honorable Minister Louis Farrakhan that November. Farrakhan invited me to his farm in Michigan, where he spoke to me about the importance of owning land and how prior to integration black folks had owned lots of it. He talked about how in the pursuit of wanting to share toilets with white people and patronize their businesses we neglected and lost our own.

From the outside looking in, buying the Holyfield house seemed reckless. But for $5.8 million it was really a steal. I don't know how much Holyfield spent building the estate but now he was in the hole for $14 million. When the bank bought the property they initially listed it for $8.2 million. I was going to make a decent profit if I sold the Seven Isles crib. More than enough to cover buying this one.

I knew I wouldn't suffer the same fate as Holyfield. The reality was I'd been smart with my money. I am no genius but I do make genius moves. One of my smartest ones was empowering my momma and sister to oversee my investments outside of music. Both of them were always somewhat involved with managing my finances behind the scenes but when Renee quit her day job and started working for me full-time the money really started piling up.

Any company I was going to partner with had to be a business that I loved personally. It had to be something I would want to represent in my music and feel comfortable supporting in everything I did. Wingstop fit the bill. I had been a longtime consumer of their lemon pepper wings—all flats, of course—and

I liked their difference from its competitors. At Hooters your money is going toward the flat-screen TVs and the waitresses' boob jobs. At Wingstop, you pay for the wings. I opened the doors to my first franchise in Memphis in 2011. Three years later I owned nine locations, with plans to triple that number in the coming years.

Renee and I had our sights set on buying the Checkers in Carol City next. When I was thirteen working at the car wash, a Checkers stood on the other side of the street. There was a McDonald's directly next to the car wash but a Big Buford was a little cheaper than a Big Mac. I was only making $30 a day plus tips so the small difference in price made a big difference to me. It was worth taking the walk across the street. Then when I was in high school Checkers was the place where my football team would go to celebrate after we beat some other school's ass. This was another local business I had a personal connection to and felt positive about getting behind.

Then I had my ownership stake in Luc Belaire. Luc Belaire was a French sparkling rosé brand owned and operated by Brett Berish, the founder and CEO of a wine and spirits business named Sovereign Brands. Sovereign Brands was the parent company of Armand de Brignac, a $300-per-bottle champagne known within the culture as Ace of Spades. Jay-Z, who'd had a stake in Ace of Spades since it was first introduced in 2006, was about to buy out Berish and take complete ownership of the brand.

I had so much respect for Hov for that play and the whole backstory behind it. It started back when all rappers were popping bottles of Cristal in their music videos. A reporter had asked the company's director how he felt about the hip-hop community embracing the brand.

"What can we do?" he said. "We can't forbid people from buying it."

Hip-hop had been responsible for millions and millions of dollars of revenue for this company and that was the thanks we got. Jay-Z pulled every bottle of Cris off the shelves at his 40/40 Club and called for a boycott of the brand. Then he went into business with Brett Berish and Ace of Spades was born. So when an opportunity presented itself for me to partner with Brett and get involved in his newest venture, Luc Belaire, I didn't need much convincing. And it took off. Today it's the top-selling French sparkling wine in the United States.

My success in life, whether it be in music or business, is not a product of me making one flawless chess move after another. I didn't get to where I am because I never took a loss. It took ten years before people embraced my music. I couldn't close the deal on every artist I wanted to sign to MMG and not every artist I did sign took off. Not every Wingstop location moved chickens the way I needed it to. I lost an endorsement deal with Reebok that year over a lyric about slipping a girl a molly in a song called "U.O.E.N.O." A few years later I received similar backlash over a comment I made about not signing female rappers to MMG because I would want to sleep with them.

I try not to entertain the Twitter mob and gossip blogs. I learned from the CO controversy that the media is more interested in creating controversy than the truth. It doesn't take much research to see that I've worked alongside female artists my entire career. Or that my mother and sister are the backbone of my empire. But some people would rather blow up one distasteful lyric or an off-handed joke in a radio interview and make me out to be someone I'm not.

Let's keep it real for a second. This is Ricky Rozay. You came to hear some real gangsta shit, right? Saying some fucked-up shit goes with the territory. My music paints a picture of a certain kind of environment. If you're going to get up in arms over every foul lyric you might want to consider a different genre. I can own up to crossing the line and saying something regrettable from time to time but give me a break with the pearl clutching. At the end of the day my actions are what define me. I can stand by those.

Let me get back to what I was saying. I have taken my share of losses. There have been plenty. But I never let them break me. When you are chasing a dream you most definitely will be challenged. You are going to fuck things up so bad and everybody and their momma are going to tell you to quit. Success comes from saying "Fuck it. I ain't through just yet" and then giving it another go. Resiliency is what breeds success.

As I was closing on the Holyfield House I was putting the finishing touches on *Mastermind*. The title for my sixth album had come from conversations I'd been having about Napoleon Hill's Mastermind Principle. Jabbar had put me onto Hill's book *The Law of Success*, one of the books he'd read while he was locked up. Jabbar had just come home from his second trip to the feds. He had been home for two years after serving the ten year sentence he caught in '98 before he caught another case out of Arizona. I prayed this time my homie was home for good.

I set the stage for *Mastermind* with my sixth collaboration with Jay-Z, "The Devil Is a Lie." Originally I'd wanted to get Hov on another beat, a record produced by Boi1da and Vinlyz that's now known as "FuckWithMeYouKnowIGotIt." But when Jay heard the beat he liked it so much he wanted to keep it for himself. Hov was working on his first solo album in four years—*Magna Carta Holy Grail*—and he had blessed me with so many timeless verses over the years I had to let him have it. Honestly I was excited to finally get a placement on one of his albums. Of course he returned the favor tenfold with "The Devil Is a Lie."

I had to pull a similar move to get "Mafia Music III" on *Mastermind*. That was a joint I initially wrote for Dr. Dre while he was working on *Detox*. I wrote verses for him and myself and the rumor was Dre was going to get Rihanna to do the hook. But the other rumor I was hearing was that *Detox* was never coming out.

Khaled and I are fans of island music and we were stuck on this joint. If Dre wasn't doing anything with it then I had to have it for *Mastermind*. I wanted to double down on the beat's dancehall vibes and get some real Jamaican artists—Mavado and Sizzla—on there. Khaled hit Bink!, the beat's producer, who got the green light from Dr. Dre for me to keep "Mafia Music III."

Puff was the final piece of the *Mastermind* puzzle. Two weeks before the album was due I visited the big homie at his crib on Star Island. I needed to get him to sign off on "Nobody." "Nobody" was a remake of "You're Nobody (Til Somebody Kills You)," the ominous outro to Biggie's final album, *Life After Death*. The idea for the song came about during a studio session with French Montana. I'd wanted to touch on the recent attempts on my life but I couldn't address it directly. I knew too much. I wanted to come at it ambiguously like how you never knew for sure if Big was talking about Tupac on the record.

I'd already reached out to D-Roc, Big's right-hand man who was in the car with him the night he got killed. He gave me his blessing. Now I needed two things from Puff. The first was sample clearance. I wasn't worried about that part. I knew Puff was going to love what I did on there. The second thing I wasn't so sure of. One of Puff's employees from Revolt had slipped me this recording of Puff blacking out on one of his artists during a session.

"You fuckin' wanna walk around with these niggas… Where the fuck is their culture? Where the fuck is their souls at? What defines you? These niggas with these fucking silly looks on their faces… YOU WANNA WALK AROUND WITH THEM

OR YOU WANNA WALK WITH GOD, NIGGA?! MAKE UP YOUR GODDAMN MIND!"

Puff is known for his classic rants but this one was up there with the all-time greats. I wanted to use it on the song. I assured Puff I'd keep the identity of the person on the receiving end of it a secret and Puff gave me the thumbs-up. He knew the people needed to hear him talk that talk.

After listening to *Mastermind* a few times I asked Puff what he thought was still missing. He told me all the pieces of a classic album were already there. I just needed to make it all one piece. *Mastermind* needed to feel like it was all recorded in the same booth on the same day. As if me, Hov, Kanye, Lil Wayne, The Weeknd and everyone else involved had been in the studio together drinking and smoking while we made it. The way that albums were made in the '90s. There was only one person with the expertise and experience to get me there. I asked Puff to come on board as executive producer and help me bring the album home.

All of my prior albums had been mixed and mastered in a couple of hours. Puff's process took several days. I learned a lot watching him mix *Mastermind*. I had always been meticulous when it came to my music but I would perfect it on a song-by-song basis. Puff took a bird's-eye view of *Mastermind*. It wasn't enough for Mike Will Made It's high hats, snares and kicks to hit hard on "War Ready." They needed to hit the same as every other producers' on the album.

Mastermind came out dope and delivered numbers-wise. Between the shooting on my birthday and me getting dropped by Reebok, 2013 had been a little rocky but I felt like things were getting back on track. But there were more storms coming and my resiliency would soon be put to the test.

On June 21, 2014, I was scheduled to perform at Hot 107.5's Summer Jamz festival in Detroit. But when we pulled up to the venue the gates were padlocked and there were a lot of niggas standing around. The show promoter spoke to Pucci, who was in the car in front of me. After a brief exchange Pucci called our car and said that we were going back to the casino to hang out while the promoter sorted out some issue. We left and I didn't think much of the situation until we got to the casino and I saw the conversation that was happening on Twitter.

It turned out a local rapper named Trick Trick had come to Chene Park with a hundred of his goons to prevent me from performing. Trick Trick had declared Detroit was a "No Fly Zone," meaning out-of-towners had to check in with him if they wanted to perform in his city. Trick Trick was not known for his music but he did have a reputation for doing sucker shit like this. He jumped Trick Daddy back in the day for "stealing his name" and beat him damn near to death. As if anyone even knew who Trick Trick was. Trick Trick must have missed the memo that I didn't do check-ins. What I didn't understand was why he turned us away if he wanted a confrontation. If you're from the jungle you don't lock the lions out. You let them in!

When Trick Trick got asked what the problem was he said that it was between him and me, but there was nothing between him and me. I wasn't sure if he was looking for a handout or just some attention but he wasn't getting either. I didn't feel the need to shoot my way into a venue to perform but I felt bad for all the kids who came out to see me that night. Those were the people that lost out.

Before I could get to the bottom of whatever this loser was upset about I had a real problem on my hands. Meek got sentenced to three to six months in prison for violating the terms of his probation. Genece Brinkley, the judge who had been obsessed with him since he caught his case in '08, claimed that Meek had violated the terms of his probation by not getting her permission to travel out of town for a show. That may have been true but the punishment seemed excessive.

It was terrible timing. Meek's sophomore album, *Dreams Worth More than Money*, was scheduled to come out in September. That wasn't going to happen now. Wale was still working on his album and I knew he wasn't going to rush his process to make up for Meek's shortcoming. The two of them were not on good terms. Days earlier a personal dispute between Meek and Wale had spilled over onto social media. It wasn't anything serious. Just a quarrel between two passionate artists and brothers. But of course the blogs were having a field day with the story and it didn't reflect well on my label.

Losing Meek's release date was one of the factors that led to me putting out two albums in the span of eight months. I'd never released two albums in one calendar year before but at the time I felt like the team needed to put some numbers on the board in what was shaping up to be an off year.

Hood Billionaire was some hard Geechi shit with a lot of good ideas. Much of the album was inspired by my love for the city of Memphis. I'd spent a lot of time there that summer opening up my latest Wingstop locations. I'd even gotten a key to the city from Mayor A.C. Wharton for bringing so many jobs to the community. The album's first single, "Elvis Presley Boulevard," was my ode to the birthplace of rock and roll and I featured the North Memphis legend Project Pat on there. Other Memphis artists like Yo Gotti and K. Michelle were on the album too.

The other element of *Hood Billionaire* was my reunion with an old friend. Kenneth "Boobie" Williams. Boobie and I had stayed in touch ever since he got locked up but this was the first time he allowed me to feature him in my music. Boobie called in from USP McCreary in Kentucky, where he's serving life, and my engineer E-Mix recorded the conversation so we could have snippets of it interspersed throughout the album.

There were dope records on *Hood Billionaire*. The problem was I didn't take the time to go through it with a fine-tooth comb the way I usually do. Take "Movin' Bass" for example. "Movin' Bass" was a record Jay-Z and I had worked on the same day we did "FuckWithMeYouKnowIGotIt" in New York. Hov did a hook during the session but he didn't get to a verse. We just had him mumbling a freestyle over the beat before we ended up having to part ways.

The turnaround for *Hood Billionaire* was so tight that we weren't able to properly revisit the song. But I wanted to do something with the record. Hov gave us the green light to use his hook but not any of his unfinished verse.

The record still sounded dope and I probably could have gotten away with having half of a Jay-Z feature if it weren't for Timbaland. Timbaland had been in the studio that day and had the files from the session. He went and leaked a version of the song that included Hov's unauthorized vocals and put one of his artists on there before my album even came out. It made it seem like his was the real version of the song and mine was a knock-off. I was so pissed at Timbaland for doing that shit.

When *Hood Billionaire* came out people could tell it had been somewhat of a rush job. It sold half as many copies as *Mastermind*. My money was at an all-time high so that wasn't what I cared about. I just didn't like that I'd let my fans down.

Mr. Ross is trying hard to find new ways to present himself, making this an ambitious album, but not always one with the right ambition.

—*The New York Times*

Ross' commercial interests, from Maybach Music to Wingstop, are so fundamental to his identity (and lyrics and social media presence) it's tough to see him removing himself from the business mindset of pushing out as much content as possible... He could benefit from taking a step back and focusing on quality over quantity. For now, Hood Billionaire is a half-baked testament to how difficult it is to make great records in rapid succession.

—*Consequence of Sound*

It's sonically interesting at times on headphones and undoubtedly sounds fine on warm open roads, but these are things you could say about any Rick Ross release. Without any truly standout tracks, it's easy to call Hood Billionaire unnecessary.

—*Pop Matters*

Between in-fighting within my label, Meek getting locked up, and now the first commercial and critical dud of my career, 2014 was not the return to form I'd been planning on. And MMG wasn't looking like the untouchable empire that I claimed it to be. I was out here looking weak.

CHAPTER

18

2015 WAS SUPPOSED TO BE A REBUILDING year. At first it was shaping up to be. Wale's *Album about Nothing* came out and debuted at number one. Meek was back home after five months in Curran-Fromhold Correctional Facility. He was putting the finishing touches on *Dreams Worth More than Money*. Even wild-ass Gunplay had a release date on the calendar for his long-awaited solo album. The team was still intact. The movement was still moving.

Having just dropped *Mastermind* and *Hood Billionaire* back-to-back, I was in no rush to put out another album. The project I was most focused on at the time was myself. Over the last year I'd lost nearly one hundred pounds and there was still work to be done. Ever since the seizures, I knew I needed to start taking better care of myself. But it wasn't until I discovered CrossFit and put my own spin on it—I called it RossFit—that the pounds started to fall off.

I was eating better too. I'd hired a personal chef, Amaris, and she was making it easy for me. The first thing I did was swap out soda for water. Then Amaris started giving me this drink after my workouts that was so good I thought it was Hawaiian punch. It turned out to be beet juice infused with organic fruits and a splash of lemonade. Then Amaris tricked me into eating cauliflower. She mashed it up and served it to me with short ribs. I could have sworn it was mashed potatoes. Who ever thought Rozay would be drinking beet juice and eating cauliflower? And if I just happened to go to dinner at Prime One Twelve and be in the mood for some dessert I let myself have it. A boss doesn't have restrictions. Sometimes a boss has to eat like a boss.

Speaking of Amaris, she was riding shotgun when my problems started that summer. She had just gotten to Atlanta and we had plans to go to a nursery and get a whole bunch of herb and vegetable plants. We were about to get Rozay Farms going and have all types of shit growing there. Collard green plants. Tomatoes. Cucumbers. Sweet potatoes. I really wanted to find me an Asian pear tree. Shout-out to all the pears. We had a whole day planned out. But as soon as we pulled out the house we got pulled over by the Fayette County Sheriff's Office. As Deputy Sheriff Tommy Grier stepped out of his cruiser and started walking toward us I looked over at Amaris and told her everything was going to be okay. She was already praying and clutching at her rosary beads.

Grier looked like the type of guy who liked to cut eyeholes in his bedsheets and wear it over his head when he wasn't in uniform. He told me he'd pulled me over for having illegal window tints. Too dark, he said. I knew that wasn't what this was about. I hadn't interacted with the police in Fayette County one time since I bought the Holyfield house and now all of a sudden they were waiting outside my property to check out the tints on my Mulsanne.

"Is that your house you came out of?"

"It is."

"Why does your car have Florida tags?"

"Because I live in Florida too."

"Well, you'll need to change those, Mr. Roberts. You're in Fayetteville, Georgia, now."

From there it became obvious that this was no routine traffic stop. I was cuffed and detained in the back of the cruiser after Grier said he detected the smell of marijuana and called for backup. That was a lie. There was some weed in the car—I have people driving my cars and rolling me joints literally all day long—but there was no way he could have smelled a couple of joints sitting in a plastic bag underneath the floorboard. It wasn't like I'd been smoking in the car when he pulled us over. We had just left the house.

But Grier saying he smelled weed gave him the probable cause he needed to search my car. When he did, he found the joints. He also found my Glock. I had an active license to carry firearms so that should have been no problem. But from the look on Grier's face I could tell he was excited by his discovery.

Amaris started crying when a female officer arrived on the scene and put her in handcuffs. I could see her knees buckling. I don't think Amaris had ever gotten so much as a parking ticket. That's when I started going bad on Grier. I'd told him Amaris had nothing to do with anything that was in my vehicle but he didn't care. Even Grier's partner, Deputy Tyler Simpson, was saying she should be let go. Simpson was another fat, thick-necked white guy but he was actually cool and respectful the whole time. Grier was the only one fucking with us. I told him he was a donut-eating fat fuck and that his wife was stepping out on him and when he found out he was going to forgive her because that's just the type of pussy cracker he is. Grier tried to talk back but he didn't have the IQ to go insult for insult with me. He was out of his league.

I talked shit to Grier the whole way to Fayette County Jail and I walked in that bitch yelling at the top of my lungs. I had to set a precedent how I was going to be treated here.

"Rozay in the motherfucking building! Which one of you fucking pigs are going out to get me some Wingstop?!"

Deputy Simpson brought me to the short-term holding cell, where he took off my cuffs. I kept telling him not to.

"Leave them on! I want Grier to take them off! Grier put 'em on me. Please have him take them off too!"

I saw Grier walk out of an office with a stack of binders a few minutes later. He started bragging to his coworkers.

"Looks like I'm all over TMZ! I guess this guy's a big-time rapper."

Fear Grier was acting like he didn't know who lived in the most famous house in Fayetteville. This guy was such a loser.

After spending ten hours in central booking I was booked on a misdemeanor marijuana charge. A few hours later I posted a $2,400 bond and was free to go. I'd met and chopped it up with a few real niggas in there so on my way out I paid their bonds too.

Amaris wouldn't get out for another twelve hours. Since I'd been arrested before, my fingerprints and information was all in the system. They had nothing on her and had to make sure she wasn't giving them a fake alias. Finally they let her go. I sent her on vacation to Paris the following week because I felt so bad about putting her through that ordeal. She was traumatized.

I was heading home but I knew whatever this was really about wasn't over yet. Two weeks later I found out.

Rapper Rick Ross Arrested on Suspicion of Pistol-Whipping, Kidnapping Employee

—*The Los Angeles Times*

Warrants: Man Assaulted by Rapper Rick Ross "Lost Use of Jaw"

—The Atlanta Journal-Constitution

Rick Ross Charged in Assault that Left Victim Unable to Chew Solid Foods

—Fayette County News

This is how it went down. Jonathan and Leo were laborers who had previously worked on one of my homes in Miami. At the time under the supervision of my general contractor, a guy named Garabello.

When I bought the Holyfield estate, Garabello moved up to Georgia and he brought his whole team with him, Jonathan and Leo included. There was a lot of work to be done and it was going to take a while to get this place up and running. The groundskeeping had been neglected for years. The house needed renovations. Furnishing all 109 rooms was its own process.

Among his many responsibilities Black Bo served as the estate's property manager. He oversaw all the work being done and would give me updates. Because Garabello didn't know English, Black ended up communicating more with Jonathan, who was bilingual. Over time Jonathan became an intermediary between the two.

Long story short, I ended up letting Garabello go. But I kept Jonathan. Jonathan vouched for Leo so Leo got to stay too. Since neither of them were from Georgia, I let them stay at the guesthouse. I was still living at the studio house. The big house was still a work in progress and security had been an issue. We'd had incidents of folks jumping the gates. The community hadn't yet adjusted to the property being under new ownership and it hadn't been made clear that trespassing would not be tolerated. That's why I was still staying at the studio house.

On the morning of June 7, Black went over to the big house

to check on things. It was a Sunday. Nine out of ten Sunday mornings Black and I were not home. We're usually still on the road. When Black got to the house he noticed a few unusual things. The first was that nobody was outside working. The second was that an unfamiliar car was parked outside of the guesthouse. The third red flag was that the guesthouse's garage was closed. All the groundskeeping tools were stored in the garage— the lawn mowers, Weed Eaters, rakes and shovels—and it was always left open.

Black knocked on the front door but no one answered. When he went around back and tried to look inside he couldn't. A black plastic material covered the window.

He headed over to the main house, where he finally found Leo. The two of them exchanged words. Black wanted to know why nobody was outside and whose car was parked at the guesthouse. He couldn't get a straight answer out of him. Leo was evasive. He kept changing the subject. At that point Black called me and said we had a situation on our hands.

"Nobody was working when I got here," he said. "And I think they've got people staying there too."

I knew what was going on and I was pissed. These Chicos thought I was out of town and decided to have themselves a party. Not only were they not working, they had brought strangers to my home and were up to who knows what there. I immediately had Black come pick me up.

The garage door had been opened by the time we got back. I grabbed my pistol, told Black to wait outside and stormed into the house. As I made my way down the hallway I could hear activity coming from inside the bedroom. I could smell smoke and it wasn't weed. I couldn't recognize the smell. I called out but nobody answered. Then I entered the room.

Due to the taped-off windows it was dark in there. But I could see that there was a young woman that I didn't know.

She was topless. Then I felt somebody reach out and grab me from behind.

I spun around and struck whoever had just touched me with the pistol. The I hit him again. I must have got him with the corner of it because blood was pouring everywhere. That's when I realized it was Leo. He was split real bad.

The young woman started screaming, and when I turned back to her I saw that she had a little girl with her. Then I heard two more voices coming down the hallway. It was another couple and they had a child as well. Aside from Leo I didn't recognize any of these people. I started waving the gun around and told them all to get the fuck out the house. They did so in a hurry.

When I went outside Black was fighting with Jonathan. Jonathan had showed up and tried to go into the house after he heard the commotion. Of course Black didn't let that happen and punches had been thrown.

I cussed everybody out and made them leave. The whole incident went down in less than ten minutes. The next day, after my temper subsided, I had Black reach out to Jonathan and Leo to smooth things over. I was still upset by what they'd done but cracking Leo's dome open had been an accident. It didn't need to go down like that.

I don't know what Jonathan said to Black when he called. But he most definitely didn't tell him that he had already gone to the police. Or that he had told them that Black and I had dragged him back inside the house and beat him with the pistol for another ten minutes.

Three days later Deputy Grier was creeping outside my gates waiting for me. And two weeks after that twenty US Marshals descended on the studio house.

After three weeks in the hole I was now on house arrest. I was feeling paranoid. I knew that they were tracking my every move with the GPS ankle monitor, but was it possible the device was recording my conversations? My lawyer said that was impossible but even then I wasn't convinced. This case was some bullshit but it had me suspicious of everything. Especially the part involving those US Marshals. Anything having to do with the feds immediately had me on high alert.

One of the first things I remember happening while I was on house arrest was that Meek started going at Drake on Twitter. That was puzzling to me. I had a longstanding friendship with Drake and as far as I knew he and Meek did too. They'd had a huge record together a couple years back called "Amen," and Meek had just featured Drake on a song called "R.I.C.O." that was shaping up to be one of the bigger singles off his album. Now for some reason Meek was coming for Drake's neck.

Publicly Meek was saying that Drake had offended him by using a ghostwriter on "R.I.C.O." I didn't believe that. My thinking was that one of two things was happening. Either Meek was letting his nuts hang and thought he had the juice to come for Drake's crown or this was about something else. I had a feeling what that something else might be. The woman Meek and Drake both had strong feelings for. Nicki Minaj.

Nicki and I had worked together on several occasions over the years and once she and Meek started dating she would be over my house all the time. They were there the night before the feds came. Nicki was cool. I didn't have anything against her. But this was a new relationship and when push came to shove I knew Nicki would never go against Wayne and Drake. That Young Money team spirit was strong like MMG's was. I didn't want to see Meek's pillow talk get used against him. I told him to be careful.

But Lil Fish was in love and he wasn't trying to hear that from me. So I took a back seat to the situation and let it play out on its own. It didn't go well for Meek. Drake was battle-tested and war-ready and fired back with two devastating disses. By the time Meek could come up with one of his own the general consensus was that this feud was already over with and that it hadn't even been close.

Behind the scenes I did what I could to see that things didn't get out of hand. I spoke with J. Prince, Drake's big homie, and he was on the same page I was. It was nothing but love and mutual respect. But when I reached out to Birdman, Drake's label boss, I was met with indifference and dismissiveness. His guy was winning this war so why should he give a fuck about mine?

At that point I really started to second-guess my relationship with Birdman. Ever since Wayne called me from Rikers Island I'd known he wasn't being supported by Stunna. Now Wayne was suing him for more than $50 million in unpaid advances and album royalties. Meanwhile Khaled had just gotten himself out of his deal at Cash Money after years of having to pay producers out of his own pocket because Birdman refused to cut the check. T-Mix, the Suave House producer I used to work with in Greg Street's basement, had gone on to do production for Cash Money after Mannie Fresh left the label. He never received proper credit or compensation for that work.

This was not an honorable man. For a long time I turned a blind eye to that because I idolized Birdman and had so much respect for his accomplishments in the game. We'd done a whole album together at one point. But after he showed his hand with the Meek and Drake situation all of my respect for him disintegrated.

I wanted to go to war for Meek but at the same time I didn't see the need to ruin my friendship with Drake. I had a feeling the two of them were going to patch things up soon anyway.

But I wanted to make it clear I was in Lil Fish's corner and I did. So I went at Birdman instead.

> Color money got your bitch out on a world tour
> My lil homie made a million on his girl's tour
> We back to back and down to whack a nigga's unborn
> Miami niggas got 'em changing all the gun laws
> So run, Forrest, got some shooters and they dying too
> I got more money than that pussy that you're signed to

—"Color Money,"
Black Market (2015)

I wouldn't find out for another month whether I'd be allowed to travel for work while under house arrest and I was starting to go a little crazy. So I locked myself into the studio and started working on a new album, *Black Market*.

Even if I got the green light to travel I knew there would be a lot of restrictions. I wouldn't be able to properly promote an album. *Black Market* was also my last contractual obligation to Def Jam and I had a feeling they weren't going to be rolling out the red carpet for my next release. We'd made a lot of history together but our relationship had run its course. They knew I was out of there after this one.

I needed to find a way to make this album special. *Hood Billionaire* had its moments but didn't connect with fans the same way *Teflon Don*, *Rich Forever* and *God Forgives, I Don't* had. I needed to right the ship with *Black Market* as I looked ahead to major label free agency.

I thought back to 2010 and the release of *Teflon Don*. How I'd teased the album with *The Albert Anastasia EP* first and the anticipation it created after people heard "B.M.F." and "MC

Hammer." I was going to do that again. *Black Market* needed a precursor. That precursor became *Black Dollar.*

Learn to walk a tightrope
Ever seen a rich nigga go broke?
They putting liens on a nigga's things
Publicize your demise and by all means
Your family fortune is forever what you stood on
Sold dreams, fantasies that put the hood on
You reap what you sow and they speaking repossessions
To the culture itself, these are powerful lessons
These niggas always smiled when I came around
They let you know my reputation when you in my town
A real nigga, you gon' know that by the contract
Bottom line blood, show me where them ones at
That paper it get funny when publishing is involved
Mechanicals never mattered because that was your dog
Now you hands-on but things don't ever seem right
You make a call to give your lawyer the green light
He look into it then hit you up with the bad news
It's so familiar, he did the same with the last dudes
Mafioso, baby girl, cash rules
Every dollar accounted for, double M the crew

—"Foreclosures,"
Black Dollar (2015)

Black Dollar was a project that came out of a period of solitude. I wasn't traveling then. I wasn't in the clubs. I wasn't smoking. I was at home. Those circumstances brought out a different side of me. Less bravado, more wisdom. It wasn't that I made a conscious effort to make a different kind of album. It's just what was coming out of me at the time. Even the beats I was choosing were different.

The spirit of *Black Dollar* carried over into *Black Market*. Eventually I'd gotten the okay to travel for domestic shows and appearances but I was well aware that this album might be my last as a free man. If it was, then what did I want to say? What did I want my legacy to look like? That was the energy behind songs like "Foreclosures" and "Free Enterprise."

The Miami Don remains an unapologetic and indefensible brute—and he says as much on this very LP—but this rough, honest, and ambitious work is like his Raging Bull, taking the listener on a compelling, dirty journey that's also a connectable character study, and then letting some slick features play while the credits roll.

—AllMusic

The motivated, slightly weary Ross heard on Black Market *is a better fit for the moment than the bulletproof supervillain of old. Ross has proven his resilience in the past; maybe carefully controlled doses of reality are just what he needs to move forward.*

—Pitchfork

Black Market *is the first moment I can remember Ross sounding comfortable as a middle-aged rapper. He's grunting out these dense and writerly couplets, hanging out with Nas and John Legend, making the DJ Premier track he'd probably always wanted to make. He's rapping more about relationships, less about drug-dealing. He's still funny, still willing to chant about how good his dick is on a song called 'Dope Dick.' But he finally sounds like the grown-up that he's been for a long time. He's a legacy artist now. It suits him.*

—Stereogum

Two months after the release of *Black Market*, a Fayette County grand jury formally indicted me and Black on twelve felony charges stemming from the incident at my estate: two counts of kidnapping, seven counts of aggravated assault and three counts of possession of a firearm during the commission of a felony. That was when the severity of my situation started to sink in. I only needed to be convicted of one of these crimes to get a life sentence.

Considering the charges I had pending I was surprised to receive an invitation to the White House a few weeks after my indictment. President Barack Obama invited a dozen artists to Washington, DC, for a roundtable discussion about criminal justice reform and My Brother's Keeper, his initiative to empower young black brothers to reach their full potential. I was honored to be a part of that group, which included Khaled, Wale, Busta Rhymes, Chance the Rapper, Nicki Minaj, Pusha T, J. Cole, John Legend, Ludacris, Alicia Keys and Janelle Monae.

My legal troubles aside, it was perfect timing for me to meet Obama. Two weeks earlier Obama had granted executive clemency to Wayne Parker. Obama was commuting the sentences of hundreds of nonviolent drug offenders and after seventeen years in prison, Wayne was coming home. Being that I was the last person to see Wayne before the feds snatched him up, it was only right that I be the first person he saw when he got out in a couple months. I was going to pick him up and take him straight to the Mercedes-Benz dealership. I wanted my big homie to be living the same way he was when he went in. I owed Obama a debt of gratitude and I wanted to thank him personally. I also wanted to see if he could do anything for Kano. Though Kano's case was a little more complicated.

Obama was telling us about the power artists have to influence the youth in a meaningful way. What stuck with me was when he got to talking about all of his plans for after his presidency was over. This wasn't about recruiting a bunch of celebrities to get behind him so that he could get some votes for his next reelection. He genuinely cared about making a difference. I respected that. He inspired me to double down on my efforts to do the same.

Obama was talking some real shit but at some point my mind started to wander. This was so surreal. It had been ten years since I'd written the song "White House" for *Port of Miami* and now I was in the actual White House meeting with the President of the United States. I was proud of myself. I'd come a long way.

BEEP! BEEP! BEEP!

My trip down memory lane had just gotten interrupted by the sound of my ankle monitor, which was informing me that it needed to be charged. I extended my leg under the desk, hoping it would muffle the sound. But everybody in the room heard that shit go off. Secret Service agents started circling the room trying to figure out where the sound had come from. We'd all had to check our cell phones before the meeting so nobody was supposed to have anything that could be beeping on them.

BEEP! BEEP! BEEP!

Fuck.

All eyes turned to me after it went off the second time. Beads of sweat were once again forming on Khaled's forehead. Before I could acknowledge what was going on the ankle monitor lost its damn mind.

BEEP! BEEP! BEEP! BEEP! BEEP! BEEP! BEEP!

"What is that noise?" Obama finally asked. He was the first person to say something.

I raised one hand and pointed the other to my ankle.

"My bad, everyone," I said.

"Oh, you scared me there, Rick," Obama responded. "I thought this place was gonna blow!"

Everybody had a laugh at that one. But I was shaken up too. Before my daydream was cut short I'd been reminiscing about where I was when I made "White House." How I still hadn't spent a cent of my Def Jam money and was in the studio between tour stops trying to make the best album I possibly could. How I was scared of having fifteen minutes of fame and then going back to being a nobody. But I'd kept at it and I'd weathered the storms. Now my fifteen minutes was going ten years strong.

But the alarm of my ankle monitor brought my attention back to reality. It reminded me of my current situation. As far as I'd come, I was close to losing it all. And my fate would be far worse than just going back to being broke. I could be headed to the chain gang.

CHAPTER

19

TEN YEARS AFTER L.A. REID SIGNED ME TO
Def Jam I entered into a new partnership with him at Epic Records. All the labels had been interested, but I'd be lying if I
said they weren't concerned about the time that I was facing.
A lot of them wanted to see how my legal situation played out.
L.A. didn't mention it once. He believed in me now the way
he believed in me in '06 and we shared the same vision for the
second decade of my career. All the pieces were in place for me
to execute on that vision at Epic.

With my court date looming I tried to remain focused on
the things under my control. I did what I always do in times of
turbulence. I turned to the music.

But as I got to work on my next album, I tried to let myself
have some fun too. I wasn't showing it but in the back of my
mind I knew I could be going away for a while. So I wanted to
make some memories. I threw pool parties and a masquerade ball

at my estate. I went parasailing in the South of France. I went to see my Carol City Chiefs win their first state championship in thirteen years. And when my buddies on the New England Patriots pulled off the greatest comeback in Super Bowl history, I made sure that I was in attendance to celebrate.

I met Bob Kraft at a party in the Hamptons a few summers back when he introduced himself and showed me he had a "Rick Ross" Pandora station on his phone. He had a younger girlfriend who had put him onto Rozay. A year later, when the Patriots beat the Seahawks in the Super Bowl, I performed at their victory party. I had old man Kraft onstage turning up to "Ima Boss." This time around the Patriots had come from behind to beat the Falcons and Rob Gronkowski and I had ourselves a night. He and I took over Foxwoods Casino in Connecticut and got white boy wasted.

Both of us had been day-drinking. Gronkowski had been spiking beers in Boston for the championship parade. I'd been at another event where I'd been sipping some Luc Belaire. But when we linked up at the club that night I switched over to the Bumbu rum. Then I started going back and forth between the brown liquor and the rosé. That's when I started to feel different.

We had been spraying champagne into the audience so Gronk had a towel covering his laptop to keep it from getting wet. At some point I realized I was going to need to borrow that towel. Immediately.

"Let me hold that towel real quick," I told him.

"Oh, sorry bro. I need this to keep the laptop dry."

"Man, give me that fucking towel."

Five seconds later I squatted behind the DJ booth and puked my guts out. Then I stood back up, grabbed my microphone and got back to performing like nothing happened. This happened several more times until Gronk came down to check on me. He didn't seem to care that he was standing in a puddle of my vomit. He just wanted to make sure I was straight.

"Whoa! Hey! You want me to announce that you're throwing up everywhere?" Gronk asked. "Everyone will go crazy!"

"Nah, Gronk," I told him. "Please don't do that."

A month later, on my daughter's birthday, I released *Rather You than Me*. Whereas *Black Market* had been a showcase of my intellect, *Rather You than Me* turned into an album of me getting shit off my chest.

I touched on a lot. The Meek/Nicki/Drake situation. The shady dealings of my former entertainment lawyer. How Gucci Pucci and I had decided to go our separate ways.

Most notably, I addressed my issues with Birdman on "Idols Become Rivals." Even though the blogs had a field day with it, the song wasn't even on some dis shit like it was when I came at him on "Color Money." It was me sticking up for Wayne, Khaled and Mannie Fresh and expressing my disappointment on the deterioration of our friendship. "Idols Become Rivals" was some big boy rap. I once had problems with Chris Rock, but I featured him on the song to show that you can make peace with former enemies as well. I think that might have gone over people's heads but that was what I was going for. Overall, when the album came out, people seemed to understand the message and the space that I was in.

Nine albums removed from anonymity, Rather You than Me *secures Rick Ross' slot within the list of Top 5 rap soloists to emerge from the South over the last 20 years, and is among his more cohesive bodies of work to date.*

—XXL

Rather You than Me *plants itself somewhere off the Atlantic coast, on a yacht with saxophones and fine linens and Michael McDonald. The perplexing and endlessly impressive thing here is that while this style has mostly fallen out of vogue, it still suits Ross incredibly well. From the grand, contemplative 'Scientology' to the velvety 'Santorini Greece,' the record frequently sounds more foreign than it really is, like a love letter to the long-ago Obama years...* Rather You than Me *is an album that's comfortable in its middle age.*

—Pitchfork

Finally talking it like he walks it, the rapper hits a powerful stride on his ferociously articulate ninth album.

—The Guardian

The following week Black and I were back in the Superior Court of Fayette County for pretrial. Our first judge had lost his post so we had a new one presiding over the case. The Honorable Fletcher Sams. I didn't know anything about Mr. Sams but as I watched him and Steve Sadow interact I got the impression they had a good rapport. Sadow was going into *Matlock* mode. This was the shit I'd been waiting to see.

There was a new assistant district attorney there on behalf of the state and plaintiffs. Michele McCutcheon. McCutcheon was a black lady, and at first I'd thought having her as prosecutor might be to my benefit in this racist-ass county. But McCutcheon had shown no interest in discussing any type of negotiation. And after seeing how shit was playing out with Meek I knew I couldn't rely on that. Genece Brinkley was a black woman too and she was sending him back to prison every chance she got.

The state's case against me relied on the discovery of the 9mm Glock that I had pistol-whipped Leo with. They found his blood on it. But the seizure of that firearm had come from Deputy Tommy Grier's "routine traffic stop" and that traffic stop had been some shady shit. Now Grier had some explaining to do if the prosecution wanted to use the gun as evidence. I had been looking forward to seeing Sadow cross-examine this pussy and he didn't disappoint. The first matter of business was why he hadn't turned on his camera.

"Corporal Grier, let me start by playing a video that I've marked as Defense Exhibit Number 23. This has been stipulated into evidence, and it is not your dashcam video. We'll get to that in a little while. This is Fayette County Deputy Sheriff's Office Adams's dashcam."

"Okay…"

"Can you give us—so you can explain, before we go further with this—how difficult was it, on June the 10th, at 1:30 in the afternoon, for you to put on your video camera on your car? What did you have to do?"

"Objection as to relevancy," McCutcheon interjected.

"Overruled," said the judge.

Sadow continued.

"What did you have to do?"

"I would have to reach over to my laptop, use the mouse pad, the built-in, run the cursor over and click Start."

"That's it? We're talking thirty seconds?"

"Correct."

"And if you had done so, we would have, potentially, a video recording of your interaction with Mr. Roberts and Mr. James on that occasion, right?"

"We would've had video, yes, sir."

"And we also—if you had the mic on, you would've also have had audio of your interaction with Mr. Roberts and Mr. James on that occasion, correct?"

"Yes."

"But we have neither?"

"Correct."

"Because you chose not to use the video camera?"

"I did not activate my camera, that is correct."

This shit was heating up. Fear Grier was squirming in his seat. Sadow was in the zone.

"You're pulling over a Bentley. How often have you pulled over a Bentley in Fayette County?"

"Fayette County? Not often."

"As in never before this?"

"Probably never."

"Okay. So you've pulled over a Bentley in Fayette County on June the 10th. Did you have any idea, at the time that you saw the Bentley, who the driver might be?"

"No."

"None?"

"I didn't even know who Rick Ross was."

"And you didn't see it come out of the property which would be considered the Holyfield estate?"

"Yeah, I saw it come out."

"You saw a Bentley come out of the property of the Holyfield estate, but you didn't know that it was Rick Ross, or you didn't know who the current owner was of that property?"

"I heard who the owner was, but—"

"Well, who did you hear the owner was?"

"Rick Ross."

Boom. Sadow had caught him lying within the first two minutes of their exchange. Of course he'd known it was me.

"I'll pause it right here just to ask another line of questions very quickly. You said that—I think I wrote down that you had heard or knew a little bit about another case?"

"Correct."

"When we say a little bit about another case, are we talking about a little bit about another case that could involve Mr. Roberts, also known as Rick Ross?"

"Yes."

"Did you hear about or know about a little bit about that case before you pulled over this Bentley?"

"Yes."

"And what is it that you heard or knew about this case?"

"That there was some sort of a disturbance. I knew nothing about the interior of the case or anything like that."

"But you knew it involved Mr. Roberts?"

"Yes, sir."

"And you knew Mr. Roberts at that point owned the Holyfield estate?"

"Correct."

"And you saw the Bentley come out of the Holyfield estate, correct?"

"Yes."

"By the way, what was the odor that you smelled?"

"Marijuana."

"Well, just burnt marijuana? Raw marijuana? What was your—"

"As it states in my report, marijuana."

"I know. I understand what your report states. I'm asking you, did you smell raw marijuana or burnt marijuana?"

"I smelled green, unburned marijuana in the vehicle."

"So that would be raw marijuana?"

"Correct."

"All right. So let's see—"

"Which is what I found inside the vehicle."

"Oh, I know what you found. I'm asking you what you smelled."

Sadow was getting so sadistic with it that the district attorney had to step in and save him.

"Judge, I'm going to object, Your Honor, to the argumentativeness."

"Sustained."

"All right. So if I understand correctly, we're not talking about burnt? We're talking about raw, correct?"

"Yes."

"Okay. So you were able to smell raw marijuana from the moment that the front driver's window was opened?"

"Yes."

"This raw marijuana ultimately being in a plastic bag, in five joints, on the floorboard of the passenger side, correct?"

"Yes."

"And that's why I'd like to bring in the sack and the marijuana cigarettes, to see—for purposes of the record, to allow the Court to deem whether it can smell raw marijuana."

"That would be hard to determine if you're dealing with marijuana that's two years old, trying to smell it out of a bag in a different area."

"Well, but that will be up to the Judge to decide, whether he wants to do it."

"I'm just saying—"

"But your claim is that you were able to smell five joints in a plastic bag on the floorboard of the passenger compartment of the vehicle?"

"Yes. An opened, non-closed CVS plastic bag that you normally pick—you know, that you carry items out of. It wasn't sealed. It wasn't in a closed container. It wasn't sealed tight with mustard seed around it to try to hide the smell. It was just five loose marijuana cigarettes in a plastic bag."

Grier was getting desperate. Sadow had him on the ropes.

"Okay. But Mr. Roberts told you that he had smoked marijuana earlier in the day, right?"

"Yes."

"Did you smell it on him?"

"Not that I noted."

"All right. So the man that told you he'd smoked marijuana

earlier in the day, you didn't smell anything on him at all? But you could smell the raw marijuana from the floorboard of the vehicle; is that correct?"

"I advised I did not note it in my report. I cannot tell you if I smelled it on him or not on him. I am advising I did smell it in the vehicle."

"Okay. When you say you didn't put it in your report, or it's not in your report, you started this off on direct examination, and I think I noted this, was that you were required to file reports?"

"Correct."

"Right?"

"Yes."

"And I assume, having been in the business for some twenty years, that you understand that when you do such a report, you are supposed to put down all material, relevant information, correct?"

"Correct."

"And the reason you do so is because some defense counsel, such as myself, is probably going to take that report and start asking you questions about it, right?"

"Yes, sir."

"So if you'd have smelled burnt marijuana, or anything on Mr. Roberts that smelled like marijuana, you would have put that material, relevant fact in your report; would you not?"

"I would've tried to, yes, sir."

"I don't understand what you mean by 'try to.'"

"Well, because in twenty years of doing this, there are certain times that you do not put something in a report that you meant to. And if it's not in the report, I'm not going to testify to it. So if you ask me about something and I can't specifically remember it, it's not written in this report, I can't testify to the yes or no of it. I can testify that if it's not in my report, I cannot give you a yes or no answer."

"But it's not there; we agree with that?"

"Correct."

"Nor is there any mention of blood, is there?"

"No."

"Not one word in your report about noting blood on any gun, correct?"

"Correct."

"Now, wouldn't you agree with me that that is a highly relevant material fact that one would include in the report, correct?"

"Not in this report."

"Not in this report because you didn't put it in the report?"

"It didn't need to be in this report. It had nothing to do with this case."

"But let me suggest that maybe you're incorrect with that..."

Sadow had gotten surgical with it. He'd picked Grier apart piece by piece starting with the dashcam, then the detection of marijuana, and finished with the seizure of my firearm. Every step of the way there had been negligence and malfeasance on Grier's part. There had been a pattern in behavior, and the way that Sadow laid it all out, it was hard to ignore the racial component. I had to tip my hat to him. It was a thing of beauty.

When we were back in court the following week, Sadow turned his attention away from the officers' misconduct during the traffic stop to the alleged victims of this case. That was when things really started to go my way.

As soon as I was arrested they had gone and filed a civil suit against me. Bad chess move. That gave Sadow access to information he would not have had access to otherwise. Motions filed. Affidavits filed by the plaintiffs. Depositions. Interrogatories. When Sadow started going through all the filings he found statements that contradicted parts of the story originally given to the police. And he realized that the civil lawyer and the state prosecutor were not in sync. There had been no coordination between the two teams and now there were witnesses giving statements in the civil suit that went against the ones given in my criminal case.

When Sadow started admitting all those civil filings as evidence, it was a play that the prosecution wasn't prepared for.

"As the State knows, these were turned over in civil discovery by the plaintiffs to the defendants and civil defendants…" he started.

"Judge, the state is not a party to the civil proceeding, so we still oppose subject to authentication," McCutcheon responded.

The judge hadn't known about the filings either.

"You need to refresh my memory. What civil proceeding are we talking about?" he asked.

"Oh, really?" Sadow said. "Zamudio, Arias, Alexandra Henao, Oscar Henao and Ceceras have sued Rick Ross and Nadrian James."

"In what jurisdiction?"

"In the State Court of Fayette County."

The judge called for a break after that and recommended the prosecution and defense meet in his chambers. For the first time they were open to discussing a plea deal that wouldn't involve me going to prison. Whether I would beat this case at trial was still up in the air but one thing was becoming clear. If this did go to trial, Fayette County and the victims were not going to come out of it looking good regardless of the outcome. Between officer misconduct and the diminishing credibility of the plaintiffs, it was in everybody's best interest to wrap this shit up. The plan to make an example out of me had unraveled.

"Look, I'm not sure how I got this opportunity but you've got to take it," Sadow said. "You're going to plead no contest to five misdemeanors. No jail. Five years of probation."

But I'd been indignant about the case since my arrest. I'd said so much foul shit to Grier and during my time on house arrest I would be on my Snapchat sending my fans after Miss McCutcheon. I wasn't interested in accepting anything less than complete exoneration. I'd spent all this money on lawyers and I knew how bad probation could jam niggas up. Weeks earlier Meek had gotten arrested in St. Louis and I knew he was going to have to do some time for violating his parole. I wanted to walk away from this shit scot-free.

Sadow looked like he was ready to pull the last few remaining hairs out of his head. As far as he was concerned, he'd just gotten me the deal of the century. At worst I had been looking at life in prison. On a perfect day, if all the stars aligned and everything went my way, Sadow had thought he could get me felony probation. But misdemeanor probation? I had a better chance of hitting the Powerball. And here I was telling him that wasn't good enough and that I wanted to try my luck at trial.

Things were getting heated so Sadow asked everyone to leave the room except for me, Black, my momma and Renee. That's when my momma put an end to the conversation.

"You are going to take the plea deal, Will," she said. "Let's go home."

In that moment all my resistance melted away. What was I trying to prove and to who? The people I cared about most wanted this to be over. Between the seizures and the shootouts, I'd put my momma through a lot these last few years and she'd spent the last two worried sick that the feds were going to take away her only son. I knew I was the reason she'd started taking medication for high blood pressure. I could do the five years probation. I'd have to be careful as far as the weed and having guns around but we could figure that out.

"They offering the same deal to Black?" I asked Sadow.

"Yes."

That solidified my decision. Black was already a convicted felon, so if we were found guilty, our sentences were not going to look the same. Any leniency I might get for being a first-time offender would not be extended to him. I looked over at Black and he gave me the nod of approval. We went back into the courtroom and took the deal.

"Your Honor, it is the State's understanding that we were in the midst of the Defense motions to suppress. The State presented evidence both last week and most recently today. During the recess for the afternoon, the parties have been in negotiations. It is the State's understanding that the Defense have indicated they are no longer going to proceed. I take it that, then, as a withdrawal of the motions to suppress and the motion for immunity as to Defendant William Leonard Roberts."

Ha! McCutcheon was trying her hardest to spin this as a win for the prosecution. As if getting us to withdraw our motions to suppress evidence was some sort of victory. At that point Sadow stepped in and made it clear what was happening.

"Well, Your Honor, we are asking the Court to stop the hearings on the motion to suppress and on the immunity hearing because we have worked out a negotiated *nolo contendere* plea to certain charges to replace the need to go forward with the hearing. When the Court, if the Court, chooses to accept the pleas as negotiated, we will withdraw the motions."

What Sadow should have said was that his client Renzel Ravioli had just beat the case. He should have said that nothing sticks to the Teflon Don. We went home, popped a bottle of Belaire and snipped off my ankle monitor. My shackles were off.

CHAPTER

20

I'VE REPLAYED THE NIGHT OF DECEMBER 7, 2017, in my mind so many times. I do it in search of answers. To figure out what I missed or what could have been done. I never find that clarity. All I can dig up are the mundane details.

That night was the first time I ever took an Uber. I was booked to perform at a club called Rockwell in Miami Beach, and on our way the van blew a tire. Short Legs stayed with the van and waited for AAA and Black called us the Uber. It was like when I didn't know what Twitter was. It's hard to keep up with all this shit.

It was the week of Art Basel so the city may have been a little more turnt up than usual but for the most part it was a regular night. We got to the club, gave the people what they came for, picked up the back end and headed home around 4:00 a.m. I had an event at Checkers the next day so as soon as we got back I smoked me a joint and went to sleep. When I rack my brain looking for something out of the ordinary, all I can come up with is that Black was standing in a different part of the club than he usually did.

Black would always come into my room at 8:00 a.m. to give me my medicine. But he didn't come that morning. I called his phone around 8:30 but he didn't answer. When I walked over to his bedroom he wasn't there. I looked outside but all the cars were there. Maybe he took one of the Ubers to go meet up with a hoe late-night.

I called Short Legs and told him I needed him to stop and grab me a pair of Air Forces before he came to the house. The chain of command for things like that usually went me to Black to Short, so right away Short knew something was off.

"Okay, no problem," he said. "Everything straight?"

"I think so. You talk to Black? He ain't answering his phone."

"Nah, I ain't heard from dog yet."

Short got to the house with the sneakers around 10:30. We had to leave to go to Checkers soon and there was still no word from Black. We called Kane.

"You talk to Black?"

"Not since last night."

This was so unlike Black. If this had been Slab, I wouldn't have gotten worried until he was gone for a month. That's Slab. But Black didn't do shit like this. Especially when we had some-where to be.

Short thought Black might have gotten drunk and passed out by the lake so he was fitting to ride around the neighbor-hood and see if he could find him. But right before he left he noticed some clothes on the floor of one of the bedrooms. No-body was staying in that room and Short had just straightened it up the day before.

The room was empty but somebody had been there. Short went to check the bathroom and he saw vomit in and around the toilet. When he pulled back the shower curtain he found him. Black was laid out in the tub.

"Man, you sleeping in the tub?! Come on, bro, we gotta go!"

Black didn't answer and when Short grabbed his leg to wake him up he realized Black's leg was cold. He put his hand under his nose. Black wasn't breathing.

Short ran downstairs where I was getting ready to go with my two security guards, Tank and Jerry.

"Dog upstairs!" Short yelled. I knew something was wrong. I don't think I ever heard Short raise his voice like that before.

"What you mean?"

"Black is upstairs! He ain't right!"

Short called 911 and we all ran upstairs. The operator told him an ambulance was on the way and to start performing chest compressions. Short did them until he got tired and then Jerry stepped in. Jerry is much bigger than Short so we thought maybe his would be more effective. Nothing.

When the paramedics arrived they kicked everybody out of the room. I was still in complete denial of what was happening. I was sure that they were going to come out in a few minutes with Black on the stretcher. He'd give us the thumbs-up and then we'd all head to the hospital and figure out what happened.

But they weren't bringing Black to the hospital. That reality started to dawn on me when the paramedics came out of the bathroom and Black wasn't on the gurney. One of them went outside to the ambulance and came back with a body bag.

"What y'all doing?! Ain't you gonna revive him?"

"We're sorry. He's gone."

I woke up to my brother Black Bo in the tub
No pulse, still seeing posts from the club

—"I Still Pray,"
Port of Miami 2 (2019)

Everything after that is a blur. I was in shock. Short Legs, despite having just found his best friend dead, had the presence of mind to try to manage the situation. He was trying to keep this from getting out. He knew as soon as it did it was going to be total chaos. But it was too late for that. Everybody's phones were blowing up. First Black's. Then ours. My sister had called Black's son D'vante and he'd called Kane and Quise, who showed up to the house a few minutes later. I don't even want to know how they got past the gates because in that moment some poor security guard could have very easily gotten killed trying to keep them from coming in. When they got to the house the police were trying to keep them out too. It's a miracle they didn't get hurt either. Quise looked like he was seconds away from passing out. I was pretty close myself.

The medical examiner determined that Black had died of heart disease at forty-five years of age. His arteries were clogged. I don't know how much Black knew about his cholesterol or any other health conditions but I do know he wouldn't have told me about it regardless of how much he knew. Black had gotten real sick a couple years before and he didn't tell anyone until Short Legs found him all fucked up and had to rush him to the hospital to have emergency surgery. That's how Black was. He took care of so many people but he wouldn't let anybody take care of him. He didn't want to be a burden.

I do know Black drank Red Bulls religiously. Every time we'd go to the store he'd come out with two Red Bulls, a Snickers bar, a pack of sunflower seeds and some Backwoods. So Black did not have the healthiest habits. But neither did I. That scared me.

But why the fuck was Black in the tub? I had never seen him in that room. He would always either sleep in his room or on the couch downstairs.

We'll never know for certain but Short Legs may have solved the mystery. Like I said, if Black knew he was sick he would not have wanted me to know. Our rooms were next to each other so I would have heard if he was in his room throwing up or gasping for air. Short figured Black must have gone across the hall because he didn't want me to hear what he was going through. That broke my heart but I think Short was right.

This was not the first time I'd lost a close friend. In 2010 my homie P-Nut was killed in a home invasion. Two gunmen were waiting for him outside his house in Miramar as he was coming home from a Christmas party. He gave up the money but it wasn't enough. They shot him dead in front of his wife and three sons.

P-Nut was one of my best friends, but it was always understood that he was a family man first. Regardless of what I had going on, P-Nut was going to drop Raymond, Raynard and Raymelle off at school and Tameka off at work every morning. He was going to pick them all up in the afternoon too. He might get back up with me after but at the end of the night he was going home to them. They came first.

Like Nut, Black was a proud father of three. D'vante, Nadaja and Khaniyah were most definitely the apples of his eye. Everything he did was for them. But unlike P-Nut, Black never really left my side. He was the first person I saw every morning. He'd come upstairs to get me up and then we'd start our day together. Whatever I was getting into, Black would be right there with me. He was my shadow.

Throughout our court case the prosecutor always referred to Black as my bodyguard. I didn't like that. Black would be the first one to buck shots at any threat that came my way and he'd done so on several occasions. But he was so much more than hired muscle. To call him my bodyguard felt wrong.

No amount of money could buy the loyalty Black had to me. Our bond was established long before I had him on the payroll. Our friendship preceded that by fifteen years. He was my true right hand. So it wasn't just that I was going to miss him like how I missed P-Nut. I *needed* Black. I didn't know how to live without him.

But the Lord has blessed me with many great friends. After Black passed everybody stepped up to fill the void he had left in all of us. I was lucky to have Tomcat and Short Legs with me when I had another seizure three months later.

This one was different. I'd caught a cold the day before and had a bad cough. I'd been taking DayQuil and using Vicks VapoRub all day. When I went to bed that night I had a seizure. But I didn't come out of it the way I usually do. My breathing was all fucked up. At around 3:30 in the morning the girl I was with went downstairs and told Tomcat I had shit myself and was foaming at the mouth.

"911, what is your emergency?"

"I have a friend of mine. I'm at his house. I'm trying to wake him up. He's breathing hard and throwing up. William Roberts. I need an ambulance ASAP."

"He's breathing hard and unable to wake up?"

"He's breathing hard and throwing up it looks like. I know he done had seizures before. He took his medicine earlier but he's not breathing right."

"Are you with the person right now?"

"No, I'm not with the person right now. I'mma go upstairs."

"How old is he?"

"He's forty-three. William Roberts."

"Is he awake?"

"He's in and out."

"Is he breathing?"

"He's breathing hard."

"Is he completely alert?"

"No, he's not alert. He's not speaking back."

"Is he clammy or having cold sweats?"

"Yeah, cold sweats. He's breathing real hard."

"Does he have asthma or other lung problems?"

"I don't think he has asthma. He's been taking medicine. He's been shaking real bad."

"Does he have asthma or other lung problems?"

"I said don't know!"

"No problem, sir. Help is on the way. We do have paramedics responding. From now on don't let him have anything to eat or drink."

A few minutes later I was able to get myself out of bed. I still wasn't breathing right but I got into the shower to clean myself off and try to get myself together. When the paramedics and police arrived I had Tomcat turn them away. I'd been through this before. I'd be straight. But then I started coughing up blood in the shower. That had never happened before.

At that point Tomcat said I needed to go to the hospital. Short Legs came and took me to the closest one, where the doctors discovered I had aspiration pneumonia. Something had gotten into my lungs while I was having the seizure and caused an infection. I was sedated and hooked up to a breathing machine.

I'd gotten hospitalized for something similar a year before. We kept it under wraps and it never made the news but it was serious. What happened was after I took my plea deal in April I'd hit the road hard. As usual, hitting the road heavy resulted in me getting less sleep and my immune system being compromised. You can guess what happened next. On a flight home from Europe I had a seizure. I was in the hospital for a week.

This time the doctors were more concerned. Because I'd just gotten back from performing in Nairobi, Kenya. They were worried I may have brought back some sort of virus from Africa and wanted to put me under quarantine.

When my momma got to the hospital she took over the situation like she always do. She didn't trust this place to treat me properly so she had me transferred to Memorial Regional Hospital in Hollywood, where they flushed my lungs with a tube and gave me a bunch of antibiotics. TMZ reported that I was hooked up to an ECMO machine but as serious as this was, it was never *that* serious. I'm no expert but from what I've heard, getting put on an ECMO is a bad sign.

So much has happened in the time since I started writing this book. I lost Black Bo and I damn near died myself. Another friend of mine, Nipsey Hussle, was murdered in the community he was rebuilding. The footage of his death and the way it was broadcast for the world to see disturbed me on a deep level. I have seen niggas die before. I know what rigor mortis looks like. And I have most definitely crossed paths with a few rats like Eric Holder in my day. But the thought of such an honorable brother like Nipsey going out like that and that being his final image made me sick. If that low-life rat thought that going to the crazy house and letting the police come get him was going to be the end of the story then he is sorely mistaken.

A few days ago a thirty-one-year-old man named Lavel Mucherson was shot to death on 37th Avenue and 207th Street, one red light away from the old Matchbox projects. They hit his seven-year-old son who was in the car with him too. When the police opened the truck and found the bodies they saw he had a semi-automatic rifle and two handguns in there. I didn't know this young man but I knew his momma. She was best friends with Jabbar's baby momma. I pray for her and her family.

The city can change Carol City to Miami Gardens or call it whatever the fuck they want to call it but that ain't changing the way of life out here. When I started writing this I wanted to paint a picture of a certain environment at a certain time.

But all of this shit I'm telling you about is still happening in real time. That's why they call it Murder Gardens.

I don't fear death but I do fear unfinished business. When my daddy died the hardest part wasn't that he was gone. He hadn't been in my life for some time. The hardest part was living with my regrets from when he was alive. There were so many unspoken words between us.

A beautiful woman named Briana recently made me a father again. Twice. We have a two-year-old daughter and a ten-month-old son together. If something were to happen to me I want Toie, Will, Berkeley and Billion to know who their daddy was. And I want them to hear it from me. The good and the bad. I just don't want to leave any words unspoken.

Those are some of the reasons I wanted to tell my story. I wanted to pull back the curtain on my life and give niggas some game while I still have the chance to. But there are so many things I can never fully explain or discuss in depth. How is it that a former correctional officer has ties to the biggest hustlers to ever come out of Carol City? How is it that after surviving all these street beefs and shootings I still move how I want to move comfortably? How is it that I live the way I do when only one of my albums has gone platinum?

50 Cent has sold more than 30 million records. How is it that while he was filing for bankruptcy and selling Mike Tyson's old mansion for peanuts I was galloping on one of my four horses across the former Holyfield estate. Do you have any idea how much it costs to take care of four horses? I spend more on hay and horseshoes than these rap niggas spend on their kids. Tell me, how is that possible?

I can't tell you. Forgive me for that. I pray that anyone who has been reading this book has been reading between the lines. There's so much being said here that's not in black ink.

When I started working on *Port of Miami 2*, my tenth album,

I wondered if the experience would give me a sense of closure. A feeling of everything coming full circle. I thought writing this book might do the same. But it felt more like hitting the reset button. It brought back all those feelings I had at the time. The hunger. The pain. The courage. The aggression. It lit a fire inside of me. My passion for music is so genuine and I know that I'm still getting better.

> I'm printing paper, boy, I even wrote a book
> I got ten million cash, what, you wanna look?

> —"Boy a Fool,"
> *Port of Miami 2* (2019)

So this isn't the end. Like Nipsey would say, "The Marathon Continues." But how do you finish telling a story that isn't over? How do you end a book when there are more chapters left? Most of the autobiographies I've read were written by people whose greatest days were in the rearview. As much as I love my horses I'm not ready to ride off into the sunset.

What if I drop this memoir and my biggest moments are still to come? God willing, that'll be the case.

I had to sit with that question for a while. I let deadlines pass because I didn't want to miss the next hurricane. But there will always be another storm to survive. I had to make peace with telling my story as it stands. And I did make peace with that. Because the truth is, what makes me a boss is not the stories that I tell. It's the ones I don't.

★ ★ ★ ★ ★

ACKNOWLEDGMENTS

I WANT TO THANK MR. MORGAN, THE JEW-
eler at the 183rd Street Flea Market, who let me stare into his
glass case when I didn't have money to buy shit. Mr. Morgan
had the Geneva watch with the diamonds for $4,500. It looked
just like the Presidential Rolex. To me it was the Rolex. He'd
let me stand there as long as I wanted and answered all my questions. When I told him I was going to come back one day and
buy that watch, he smiled and told me, "Whenever you're ready."
He didn't laugh at me or tell me to leave his store. I never did
end up buying that watch though. So if Mr. Morgan ain't dead
and he still got one of them Genevas, somebody tell him I still
want it. I can't promise I'm going to wear it. I just want to keep
it in the safe with all the others.

Neil Martinez–Belkin would like to thank:

ROSS. YOU ARE MOST DEFINITELY A REAL
theory and a little ocky. In 2006, when I was a kid stuck on *Port
of Miami*, if someone had told me that I would get to be a part of

something like this, I never would have believed them. It's still unbelievable to me. Thank you for this opportunity and thank you for being my friend. It's deeper than rap.

Thank you to Tommie and Tawanda Roberts. Without their contributions this book would not be possible.

Thank you to all of Ross's family and friends who welcomed me into their world and took the time to share their memories with me. Jabbar, Slab, Short Legs, Tomcat, Gunplay, Geter K, Sam Sneak, Young Breed, Quise, DJ Khaled, Tony Draper, Ted Lucas, Josh, Kane, E-Class, Johnny Boy, Trina, Cool & Dre, Busta Rhymes, Greg Street, Spiff TV, Block, Gino and Kano Belizaire, Wayne Parker, 30, Dallas Martin, Earl, J.U.S.T.I.C.E. League, Wale, Bishop, E-Mix, Fonzo, Trop, Liz Hagelthorn, Steve Sadow, Shateria Moragne-el, Skinny, Chicken Man, Brother Don, Carrie Roberts, Jerry, Ducky, and Toie and Lil' Will Roberts.

Thank you to Juan Madrid and Young Sav for bringing Ross and me together for our meeting of the minds.

Thank you to my agent, Robert Guinsler, for always having my back.

Thank you to Hanover Square Press for seeing the vision and providing the infrastructure to turn this story into a book.

I would be remiss if I did not thank the doctors, nurses and staff at Brigham and Women's Hospital who took care of me when I got sick while working on this book, most of all Dr. Nino Chiocca and Dr. Daphne Haas-Kogan.

Thank you to my mother and father, my grandparents, aunts, uncles, cousins—especially Victoria!—and all my friends for reminding me what it means to be family.

And to my Goldie Jane. Do you remember what I told you about Chapter Two? Thank you for seeing me through it. And for all our chapters to come.